A World of Change

BARE RUINED CHOIRS

The Fate of a Welsh Abbey

Robert M Morris

Education Officer,
Cadw: Welsh Historic Monuments

Series editor: Rosemary Kelly

CONTENTS

How to use this book 2
Ruins in the landscape 3
The medieval abbeys 4
Centuries of change 12
The storm breaks 22
'Bare walls standing' 39
Find out more for yourself ... 50
Index 51

The ruins shown on the cover of this topic book lie in a deep, wooded valley in North Wales. They are all that remain of a thirteenth-century abbey called Valle Crucis – the Vale of the Cross. The most surprising thing about old abbey ruins like these is that they have actually been ruins for over 400 years. They were all closed, and most of them destroyed, around the same time. Their closure came very suddenly in the 1530s. This topic book tells you about Valle Crucis Abbey, and what happened to it. Valle Crucis was just one of some 848 abbeys and nunneries which existed all over England and Wales when King Henry VIII came to the throne in 1509. Their story is important because the abbeys' fate was linked with religious changes which spread all over Europe at this time. The story of Valle Crucis should also help you to judge how and why a way of life, which many people had followed for hundreds of years, suddenly disappeared from England and Wales.

Stanley Thornes (Publishers) Ltd

How to use this book

The ruins of Neath Abbey, in South Wales, about 200 years ago

Its last abbot played an important part in the closing days of Valle Crucis Abbey.

What happened to all the abbeys within the space of just a few years? In 1534 there were about 848 monastic houses in England and Wales. By 1540 there were none at all. Why did this dramatic change come about all over the kingdom? How important had the abbeys and their occupants been to people's everyday lives before that time? What impact did their sudden disappearance make? These are the most important questions that this topic book will try to answer. Most of the evidence is to be found in the writings of people who lived at the time, such as reports, official letters, financial accounts, legal papers, and laws passed by Parliament. Not all such papers, or documents, have survived the centuries. All the same, the documents that remain can help us to understand what happened. Many of the documents quoted here do not deal with Valle Crucis; there are some gaps in the records of Valle Crucis, but documents about other abbeys can help to fill these. Other extracts come from government documents which affected all the abbeys.

How can we use the different kinds of evidence available? Reports were usually written by people on official business, just like letters sent from one government to another. Many of the letters you will see in this book were written to Thomas Cromwell – Henry VIII's chief minister. Their authors had been sent out by Cromwell to inspect the abbeys, and their views often reflected Cromwell's own opinions. They often told him what he wanted to hear: criticisms of the abbeys and their occupants. Even books published at the time were one-sided. Books that disagreed sharply with the policy of Henry VIII's government were not allowed to appear.

Some comments in favour of the monasteries can also be found. Welsh poets in those days travelled from one wealthy household to another, being fed and housed in return for poems in praise of their hosts. The abbots of Wales gave them a generous welcome, and the poets showed their appreciation by reciting poems which spoke highly of the abbeys. But you must remember that their praise was often 'cupboard love' – it was not always sincere. So *you* must judge each extract quoted from the writers of the time. You must ask yourselves: does this writer have a grudge against the people being described? Does the writer hope to gain something from showing a certain point of view? In other words, is there *bias* in the extract? And are there gaps in our information – things we do not know because the evidence has not survived? Very little of the monks' own views have survived, except in official papers about the rebellions of 1536. So think about all these problems as you read this book.

Ruins in the landscape

The site of Valle Crucis abbey is ringed by green hills and towering crags, while nearby stands the small riverside town of Llangollen, world famous today for its international musical eisteddfod. Not surprisingly, these ruins have become a tourist attraction. Cadw: Welsh Historic Monuments, which cares for the site, estimates that about 15,000 people visit the ruins each year. Two centuries ago the great English artist, J M W Turner, painted Valle Crucis, looking very much as it does today, and his painting is reproduced on the cover of this book. As early as the 1580s or 1590s the great poet and dramatist, William Shakespeare, described similar abbey sites as:

> Bare ruin'd *choirs* where late the sweet birds sang.

central part of the abbey church where monks sat and sang during services

As early as 1537 a government agent named Richard Pollard wrote to London to report the ruined state of Bridlington Priory, in Yorkshire, saying that 'the house and church is far in decay'. Yet only five years before that, in 1532, a Welsh poet had written the following description of Neath Abbey, in South Wales, and its abbot, Leyshon Thomas:

> Is there a better man living than the Abbot of Neath...
> The Abbot of Abbots and their chief,
> The apple of God's eye...
> The temple of Neath, with its many new buildings
> God is glorified in these precincts...
> A weight of lead *atop* [above] the hall,
> A blue-black roof shelters the Godly...
> Through multi-coloured glasswork, glowing images
> Are cast, like shafts of sunlight
> On the monks' bright archways...
> A high, star-studded roof above
> Soars up in sight of the Archangels,
> Below, where *Babylonian crowds* [all sorts of people] parade
> The floor is paved with coloured flagstones.
> Bells, and melodious monastic worship
> Are a constant glory to the *White Monks* [Cistercians]...
> Here meat and *headstrong* [alcoholic] wine abound
> And deer *range* [wander] on the high parkland,
> While trout from the deep are found,
> There's wheat and all sorts of wines.
>
> Lewys Morgannwg

A modern artist's idea of what Valle Crucis was like in medieval times

3

The medieval abbeys

A medieval picture of monks building their own abbey in stone with a tiled roof

Making a Start

One day a small group of men trudged wearily up the hilly slopes that rose from the banks of the River Dee in North Wales. Equipped with a little food and drink, they had walked more than 25 miles, skirting the foothills of the Berwyn mountains. These were monks of the Cistercian order, and although no written record of their journey exists, it was probably made in the year 1200. The monks had come from the monastery of Strata Marcella, near the present-day town of Welshpool, on the Welsh border. A lord called Madog had given some of his land to the monks, and the abbey at Strata Marcella was responsible for setting up a new monastery on this land.

The small party's troubles were far from over even after they had forded the rushing waters of the Dee. In the remote valley of Glyn Egwestl the farming families who were already settled there had to be moved from the monastery site. The sons of Camron, of Ednyfed and of Irham, were to be given land elsewhere by Madog, who had given their valley to the monks. Philip, the new abbot, and his followers spent the first few years developing the monastery itself, and the church in particular. They lived in wooden buildings while workers quarried the stone, cut the timber and built the abbey that was now to be called Valle Crucis. To add to the monks' troubles, 1200 and 1201 were very wet years, and crops were ruined by rain and floods in many areas. The next year began with a hard winter of frost and snow, which was followed by a summer of violent storms. The monks had to get to grips with the farm-work on their new estate, but they were joined by many willing helpers who chose to live like monks without becoming full members of the abbey community. They were called lay-brothers.

Monks working on an abbey farm

The harrassed abbot Philip was accused by Church officials of neglecting religious services:

> the person mentioned [Philip] rarely celebrates Mass and stays away from the altar.
>
> From a statute, or disciplinary order, of the Cistercians in 1200

■ What reasons might Abbot Philip give for staying away from the altar in 1200?

Over the years the abbey grew and flourished. More land was given to it and more and more men joined the monastery. The religious life of the abbey may well have drawn nearer to the ideal described by Ailred, abbot of the great Yorkshire abbey of Rievaulx in the twelfth century:

> Our food is scanty, our garments rough; our drink is from the stream and our sleep often upon our book. Under our tired limbs there is but a hard mat; when sleep is sweetest we must rise at a bell's bidding... Self-will has no scope; there is no moment for idleness or *dissipation* [amusement]... Everywhere peace, everywhere serenity, and a marvellous freedom from the tumult of the world, such unity and concord is there among the brethren, that each thing seems to belong to all, and all to each.
>
> From *Speculum Caritatis* by Ailred of Rievaulx

What kind of life did monks and nuns lead? Why did people choose a monastic life? The next section will answer these questions.

Fish was an important food for monks. On Fridays fish was the only meat they might eat. Valle Crucis had its own fish weirs on the River Dee.

5

The idea of a monastery

During the early centuries of the Christian Church many Christian people found that living in everyday society, among people who did not always share their dedication made it difficult for them to give all their attention to God. They wanted to keep clear of the world's day-to-day concern with possessions and enjoyment, and to avoid life's temptations – the feeling of wanting things that distracted a person's thoughts from God. Above all, they wanted to be secure from the violence of a warlike age that made it extremely difficult for Christians to live like brothers.

For centuries many Christians went off to live in remote places alone, while others came together in groups to build a house or 'monastery' where everyone was committed to a religious life. In the sixth century an Italian nobleman named Benedict, who was himself searching for a religious way of life, brought a new, better-organised approach to living in monasteries. Many followers joined him at the abbey of Monte Cassino which he set up between Rome and Naples. He wrote a detailed instruction manual for running a monastery and for living in it. It became known as the *Rule of St Benedict* and the monks who followed the *Rule* soon became known as 'Benedictines'. Here are some of Benedict's ideas about the life of a monk:

The monks' choir singing the Latin service in the abbey church

Monks and nuns spent hours each day at services.

> This vice especially ought to be cut out of the monastery by its roots. Let no one presume to give or receive anything without the permission of the abbot or to keep anything whatever for his own, neither books, nor tablets, nor pen, nor anything else, because monks should not even have their own bodies and wills at their own disposal. Let them look to the father of the monastery for whatever is necessary and let it be forbidden for them to have anything he has not given them or allowed them to possess... Idleness is the enemy of the soul. The brothers, therefore, ought to be *engaged* at certain times in manual labour, and at other hours in divine reading... If the circumstances of the place or poverty forces them to gather the harvest by themselves, let them not be saddened on this account: because then they are truly monks, if they live by the labour of their own hands like our *Fathers* [of the Early Christian Church] or the Apostles. Let all things, however, be done in moderation because of the faint-hearted.

occupied

From the *Rule of St Benedict*

Monks were supposed to care for others and to help them:

> The whole of the day he spent... in teaching, praying, kneeling and in care for the brethren; also in feeding a multitude of orphans, *wards* [children brought up by people other than their parents], widows, needy, sick, feeble and *pilgrims* [travellers visiting important religious places].

From *The Life of St David* by Rhigyfarch, c1090

Nuns at their services in the choirstalls

Monks and their orders

The most important thing in a monk's life was the series of 'vows' he took – firm promises he made to God. There were three vows:

1. Stability: to stay in the monastery always, giving up any private possessions to become part of the monks' community;
2. Conversion of life: to change his ways, devoting his life entirely to worship, without marrying or having a family of his own;
3. Obedience: to obey the abbot or any other superiors in their order, without question.

Monastic vows were kept constantly in mind by three bulky knots in the rope-like girdle tied around the waist.

A Benedictine monk

Over the centuries many hundreds of Benedictine monasteries were built all over Europe; but later on there were different 'orders' of monks. An order was an organisation of monks with its own rules. For the tightly-organised Cistercians, each abbey would be an extra branch that enabled the order to spread like a great tree. Many new orders were established because people felt that the Benedictine abbeys had become too slack about keeping the *Rule*. Some thought they were too concerned with managing the huge estates and enormous wealth given to them by kings and lords who wanted the monks to pray for them in return. The new Cluniac order followed a pattern set by the monks at the French monastery of Cluny around the years 909–10. The monks at Valle Crucis were Cistercians and took their lead from the abbey of Cîteaux. There were many other monastic orders, and most of them had separate houses where women followed the same strict rules. The women were called 'nuns'. There were orders of 'canons' too – priests working in parish or cathedral churches who also lived in monasteries. As priests in the community, they could not live in complete seclusion. Later still, orders of 'friars' were set up. The friars did not live in monasteries; they travelled the land preaching about God and living off the generosity of the people they met, and returned occasionally to their particular 'friary' or friars' house.

A Cistercian monk

A friar on horseback

Friars were supposed to be poor and to travel on foot. A horse was a valuable property.

The monastic day

How did monks and nuns spend their time? The following timetable is based upon the standard routine, or *horarium* (hour-plan) of the monasteries. It allowed for some differences between summer and winter, and special allowances were made in later years for the colder climate and long winter nights of northern Europe compared with the Mediterranean.

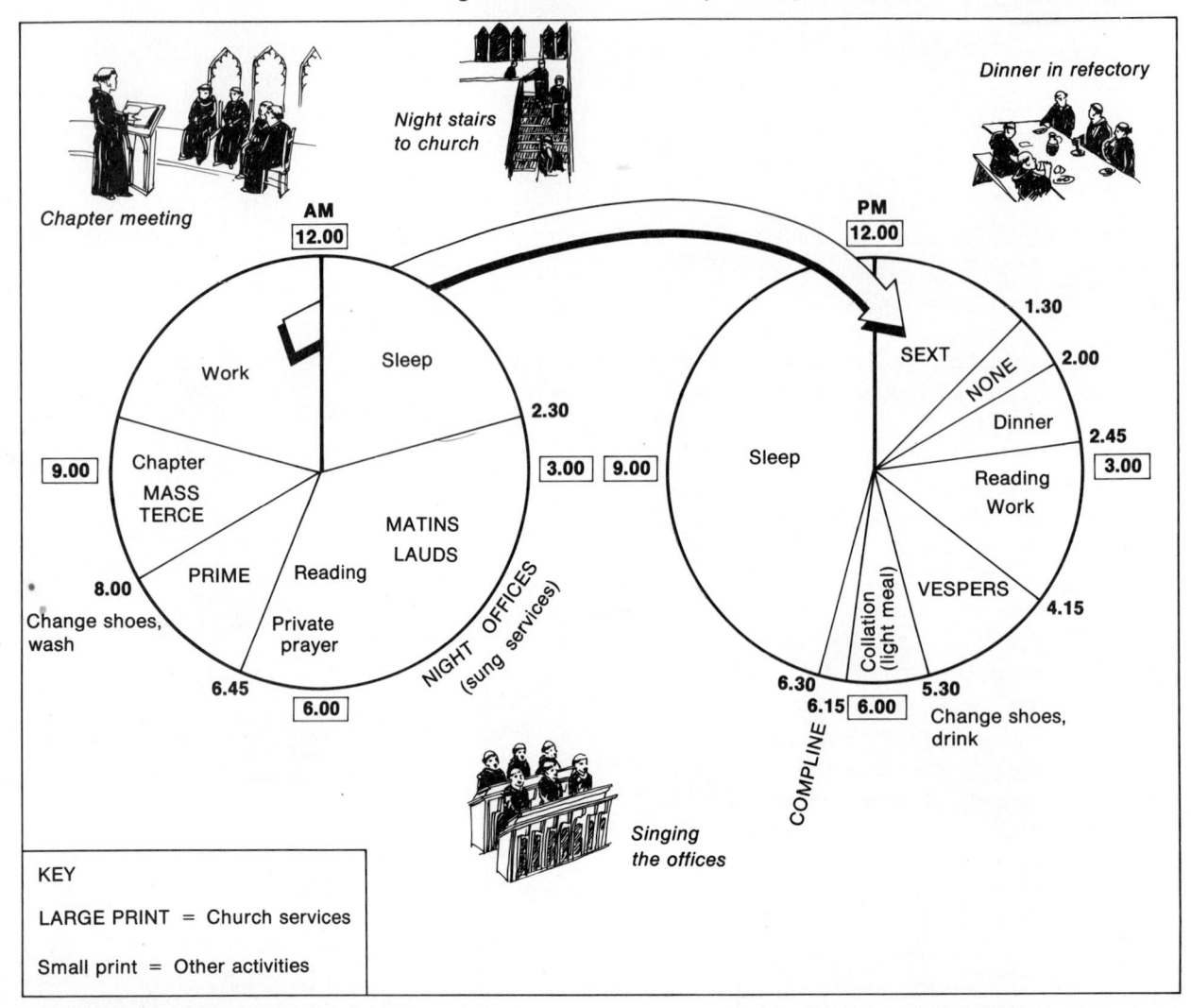

Night stairs to church

Chapter meeting

Dinner in refectory

Singing the offices

KEY

LARGE PRINT = Church services

Small print = Other activities

The monastic horarium

The monks' routine followed the available hours of daylight because they had no clocks by which to tell the time. The routine varied, therefore, from season to season. This version is based on winter hours.

■ Imagine you are a monk or nun in the Middle Ages. Think what your daily life would be like, and write a description or draw a comic strip with captions to explain how you spend your day. In a comic strip you can use 'balloons' to show what you say or think.

8

Running a monastery

Power and authority within a monastery was like a ladder leading up from the **novice** at the bottom to the **abbot** at the top. The following description from the *Rule of St Benedict* shows how important the abbot was:

> The abbot who is worthy to rule over a monastery should always remember what he is called and suit his action to his high calling. For he is believed to take the place of Christ in the monastery, and therefore he is called by His title ... 'Abba, Father' ...
>
> When, therefore, any one receives the name of abbot, ... he should display all that is good and holy by his deeds rather than by his words ...
>
> Let him show the sternness of a master and the devoted affection of a father. He ought to *reprove* [speak strongly to] the undisciplined and unruly severely, but should *exhort* [encourage] the obedient, meek and patient to advance in virtue ...
>
> Above all, let him not *slight* [ignore] or undervalue the salvation of the souls entrusted to him by giving more attention to *transistory* [lasting for a short time], earthly, and perishable matters.

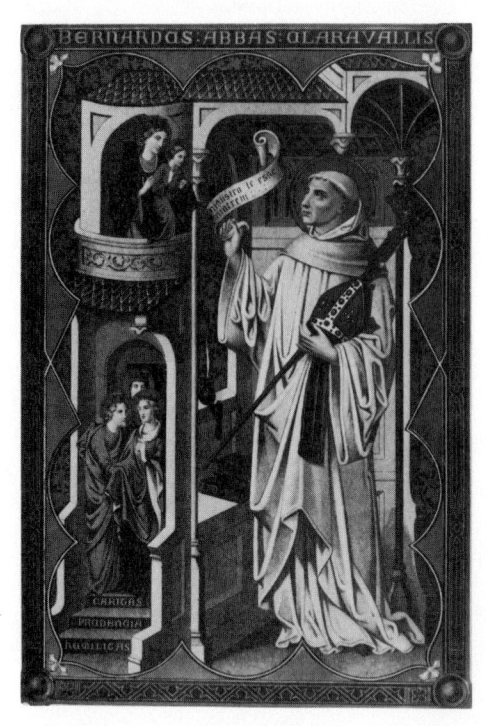

St Bernard, an important early member of the Cistercian order, preaching

The second-in-command in the monastery was the **prior**, who by the later centuries was responsible for discipline. (A **priory** would be a less important house of monks or nuns, often the off-shoot of a larger abbey. Its head would usually be known as a prior or prioress.) The **precentor** was responsible for the services in the abbey church as well as the choral singing, while the **sacrist** looked after the church buildings, the fittings and the ornaments. The **cellarer** was in control of abbey stores and food supplies – including the wine, which the cellarer shown in the picture seems to be enjoying! In the Cistercian order the cellarer became an important figure in managing the monks' estates and property. The **almoner** was in charge of the abbey's regular donations to the poor, or **almsgiving**.

Sometimes a local bishop stepped in if monastic rules were broken:

> we have convinced ourselves by clear proofs that some of the nuns ... bring with them to church birds, rabbits, hounds ... *whereunto* [to which] they give more heed than to the *offices* [services] of the church ... therefore we strictly forbid you ... that ye presume henceforward to bring to Church no birds, hounds, rabbits ... as through hunting dogs and other hounds abiding within your monastic precincts, the alms that should be given to the poor are devoured and the church and cloister are foully *defiled* [polluted] ... through their *inordinate* [excessive] noise divine service is frequently troubled – therefore we strictly command ... you, Lady Abbess, that you remove the dogs altogether.
>
> Bishop's command to the Benedictine Abbess of Romsey, Hampshire, 1387

A cellarer sampling the abbey wine

A novice's life

An abbot welcoming a novice

The ordinary monk began his career as a novice. In the early centuries children were sent to the monasteries to become novice monks, often against their wills. This had been stopped by the thirteenth century and a novice had to be at least eighteen years old. He would have a bald patch, or 'tonsure' shaved on his head to show his intention, and he wore a special novice's gown. For a whole year the young novice lived and worked like the other monks, but under the watchful eye of the **master of the novices**. At the end of the year both the novice and the abbot had to decide whether the young man was suited to a monk's life. If all had gone well, the novice took the three monastic vows, exchanged his own gown for the coarse monk's gown, or 'habit', and took the 'cowl' (monk's hood) and the knotted girdle. This is how St Benedict thought a novice's keenness to become a monk should be tested:

> Let not anyone, newly coming to the religious life, be granted an easy entrance; but, as the Apostle says: 'Test the spirits to see whether they are of God.' If, therefore, anyone perseveres in his knocking at the door, and if he is seen, after four or five days, to bear patiently the harsh treatment inflicted on him and the difficulty of admission and to persist in his petition, let admittance be granted to him.
>
> From the *Rule of St Benedict*

Although the *Rule* had originally been written for male monks, it was applied to nuns in the same way. The dress and headgear were adapted, and there was no tonsure for nuns.

Not everyone found the monastic life suitable. Some were appalled to find that fellow-monks took their vows less seriously than they themselves did. This is what Peter Abelard, a famous medieval monk, wrote:

> The abbey, however, to which I had betaken myself was utterly worldly and in its life quite scandalous. The abbot himself was as far below his fellows in his way of living and in the foulness of his reputation as he was above them in priestly rank. This intolerable state of things I often and vehemently *denounced*, sometimes in private talk and sometimes publicly, but the only result was that I made myself detested *of* them all.
>
> From the twelfth-century autobiography of Peter Abelard

spoke against

by

The novice would also be taught about the monks' role as teachers and keepers of written knowledge:

> there are those who desire to learn that they may edify others: that is charity. And lastly there are some who wish to learn that they may be themselves *edified* ... they wish to know only that they may do good.
>
> St Bernard of Clairvaux (lived 1090–1153)

taught and improved

In the mid-fifteenth century nuns at Lincoln complained to the bishop about the lifestyle of their own prioress:

> The Prioress wears golden rings exceeding costly, with *divers* [various] precious stones and also girdles silvered and gilded over silken veils and she carries her veil too high above her forehead, so that her forehead, being entirely uncovered, can be seen *of* [by] all.
>
> From a report of the Bishop of Lincoln's visitation

But more often than not the complaints were about the hard routine and the strictness of the rules. This complaint was made to the abbot of Rievaulx:

> Lord, my inconstancy is not equal to the burden of the Order. Everything here and in my nature are opposed to each other... I am tormented and crushed down by the length of the vigils, I often *succumb to* [collapse under] the manual labour. The food *cleaves* [sticks] to my mouth, more bitter than wormwood. The rough clothing cuts through my skin... More than this, my will is always *hankering after* [longing for] other things, it longs for the delights of the world and sighs unceasingly for its... pleasures.
>
> From the *Life of Ailred of Rievaulx* by Walter Daniel

Nuns in their convent

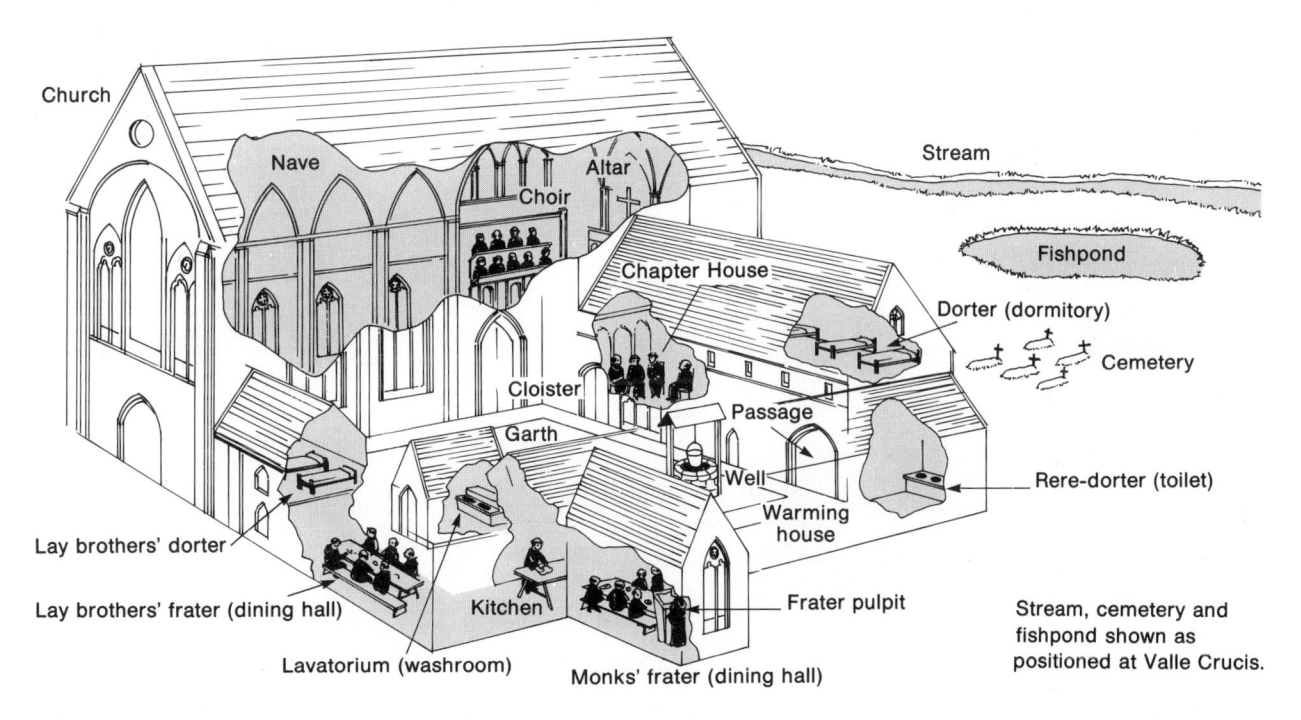

A Cistercian abbey: What it may have looked like

Stream, cemetery and fishpond shown as positioned at Valle Crucis.

1 Most monasteries were built to a plan roughly similar to the one above. Why were the different parts of the abbey laid out like this?

2 Draw a 'ladder' showing the rank (order) of monks, from abbot at the top to novice at the bottom, with cartoon figures standing on the rungs.

Centuries of change

Snapshots of monastic life

Life in the various kinds of monastic houses went on for centuries in its unhurried, orderly way. Yet there were changes, and life in the cloister was not the same in 1530 as it had been in 1230. The number of monks dwindled in the later centuries. By the time the English and Welsh monastic houses were closed there were, on average, about twelve monks in each house, though the numbers varied according to the size and wealth of each monastery. The following tables shown how many religious houses there were, and the differences of wealth between them:

A friar preaching outside a church

The friars did important work in their early years, teaching people about the Christian religion.

Religious Houses and their Occupants c1534		
	Houses	People
Monks	253	3,650
Canons	275	2,790
Nuns	137	1,908
Friars	183	2,341
Totals	848	10,689

Differences in Monastic Wealth	
	Income per year
The 5 major abbeys (Glastonbury, Canterbury, Westminster, St Albans, Clerkenwell)	over £2,000
19 abbeys	over £1,000
150 abbeys	£200–£700
Smallest abbeys	£20–£30

In the fourteenth century the number of monasteries in western Europe reached its peak, and in the year 1350 there were 1,028 religious houses in England and Wales alone. The following extracts give brief glimpses of life in some of them.

Change through time?

Knowing that carefree rest was the source and mother of *vices* [wickedness] he [Saint David] bowed down the shoulders of the monks with pious labours ... Thus they work with feet and hands with more eager fervour. They place the yoke upon their shoulders; they dig the ground unweariedly with *mattocks* [pickaxes] and spades; they carry in their holy hands hoes and saws for cutting, and provide with their own efforts for all the necessities of the community.

From the *Life of St David* by Rhigyfarch, c1090–5

Our Cellarer received all guests of whatever rank at the expense of the Convent. William the Sacrist gave and spent as he pleased, a kindly man, giving away both that which should be given and that which should not, and 'Blinding the eyes of all with gifts'. Samson the sub-sacrist, being master of the workmen, left nothing broken or cracked or split or unrepaired to the best of his power: wherefore he won the favour of the Convent and above all of the cloister monks. In those days our choir-screen was built under the direction of Samson, who arranged the painted stories from the Bible and composed *elegiac* [mourning] verses for each. He had a great quantity of stone and sand hauled for the building of the great tower of the church. And when he was asked *whence* [from where] he got the money to do this, he replied that certain of the *burgesses* [townspeople] had secretly given it to him for the building and completion of the tower.

From the *Chronicle of Jocelin of Brakelond*, c1200

A carved figure of a monk, at work with a spade

It can be seen in Worcester Cathedral, a former abbey church.

Walter Percehay of Ryton in the county of York, gentleman ... has always had the right ... to dig turf on the waste ground and common ... William Scarburgh, the finance officer of Rievaulx Abbey, with [eighteen named men] and some 30 others, assembled at Pickering to deprive [Percehay] of his right ... and using armed force and riotous behaviour, with staves, small shields and weapons, they carried away in seven wagons the turf that Percehay had dug previously.

A complaint from Yorkshire to one of the King's courts in London, 1519 (given in modern wording)

1 Which of the following monks named in the last three extracts do you think is (a) the best, and (b) the worst example of a monk's behaviour – Samson, William (finance officer of Rievaulx) or St David?

2 Would it surprise you to know that Samson (sub-sacrist of Bury St Edmund's) later became abbot? Why do you think the monks elected him?

3 These three extracts were written over a period of more than 400 years. Do the extracts show any change in monastic life during that time?

4 Draw a series of three pictures, showing scenes from each of the three extracts you have just read.

The terror of the Black Death

Two pictures of the time show how death awaited the most important people and the peasant at his plough.

Religion was very important in people's everyday lives both in and after the Middle Ages. In a hard world there was comfort in the fact that the Church was there. Life itself was very uncertain for everyone, rich or poor, and the constant shadow of sudden death hung over them in an age of plague, crude medicine and violence. This poem by the Welsh poet, Sion Cent, shows how some people felt:

religious help in spite of all his activity	Let men therefore every day To God for *ghostly succour* pray. *For all his stir* no man can know How far on earth 'tis his to go: Today a great lord set on high, Tonight in his lonely grave to lie,...
land	No poor man's *portion* shall he seize Nor revel at his lordly ease;... No fine silk shall clothe him there, Gravel's then the only wear;

Sion Cent, *c*1400–30

Apart from praying for the dead, monks provided food, or 'alms', for the local poor, as well as meals and lodging for travellers. An alms centre, or 'almonry', at Canterbury, is shown above.

■ How would you sum up in one sentence the point Sion Cent is making?

This anxiety about death made rich people give land and wealth to the Church on a huge scale. The monasteries were very important because the monks spent so much of their time praying. Whole abbeys were founded to pray for powerful people. A generous donor could hope for the monks' constant prayers while he lived, as well as prayers for his soul after death. In the thirteenth century Lord de Courtenay had given land to Forde Abbey in Dorset. He believed to the end of his days that the distant prayers of the Forde monks saved him from shipwreck, some years later, during a raging storm in the English Channel.

At Valle Crucis Abbey the monks' dormitory overlooked the abbey cemetery, where graves were kept in a half-dug state – ready for new additions at any time. One historian wrote much later in 1878, that the view from the dormitory must have been 'deplorably cheerless'. On the other hand, important lords and ladies from the surrounding districts would be buried in the abbey under carved grave slabs. Many of these slabs survive to this day. They show how widely-respected the abbey was.

Public opinion about the monks could often be seen in the lavish gifts which were given to their abbeys. Medieval people believed that the gifts an abbey received reflected public regard for it. A bishop of St David's, in South Wales, wrote to a nobleman in the twelfth century about a priory which the nobleman's family had supported:

A ship in a storm at sea

> It should indeed give you pleasure and bring you profit in God's eyes that *that house* has of late increased to a more than *customary* degree in religion and charity. Much encouraged by this, we have confirmed the gifts of your ancestors.
>
> Letter by Bishop Bernard of St David's to the Earl of Hereford

Brecon Priory; usual

1 Why was the bishop keen to give the Earl this information?

2 Imagine yourself as a monk who is being challenged by an outsider to justify his way of life as a monk. Explain why you think monastic life is both useful and worthwhile to medieval society.

3 What did Bernard mean by saying the priory had increased in charity?

Valle Crucis: Good times, bad times

The small abbey of Valle Crucis, in this secluded Welsh valley, felt its share of the swirling tides of medieval troubles. The abbey had developed well. It had been given further parcels, or portions, of land as well as the tenants' rents and the work they did in return for their land. In those days people had to pay **tithes** on their land – 10 per cent of the year's farm produce – to the Church. As four parish churches and all their incomes had been granted to the abbey, this brought a fair-sized sum in tithes to the monks. The abbey did, however, have to give back a share of the churches' income to pay for a priest in each parish. The tables on the next page show what the income of Valle Crucis abbey was in 1535 and how some of it was spent. The statistics come from the huge government survey of religious houses made in that year. It was called *Valor Ecclesiasticus* (Church Valuation). The map below the tables shows the district where the abbey's property lay, in the Wrexham-Llangollen area of Clwyd.

Valle Crucis: Where the cash came from

All monastic houses had two kinds of income. **Spiritual** income came from churches controlled by the abbey, especially tithes; **temporal** income came from ordinary property – mostly farmland. Most of their lands would be rented out to tenants, but they kept some for themselves – the **demesne**, or **home farm**. Mills, fish weirs and sometimes mines, quarries or even port-facilities on their land could bring in still more money. Law-courts in the areas controlled by the abbeys brought in fines and legal fees. Most abbeys had more temporal income than spiritual; but Valle Crucis was unusual because 75 per cent of its income was spiritual – coming from the parish churches under its control.

People paying tithes to the church

These payments were a vital part of a priest's income until this century.

Spiritual Income

Parish	Abbey's Share £ s d	Priest's Share £ s d
Wrexham	54 16 8	20 18 4
Ruabon	29 16 8	13 16 8
Llangollen	32 16 8	10 0 0
Chirk	11 15 5	6 13 4
Llansanffraid-Glynceiriog[1]	6 5 0	—
Llandysilio-yn-Iâl[1]	10 0 0	—
Bryneglwys[1]	7 5 0	—
Abbey's total (spiritual)	**152 15 5**	

Temporal Income

	£ s d
Abbey home farm	8 9 8
Abbey granges[2]	20 4 8
Llangollen mill	4 13 4
Court fees	1 6 8
Wrexham grange	14 2 8
Wrexham mill	5 0 0
Court fees	2 13 4
Chirk grange	3 19 0
Chirk home farm	1 6 8
Total (temporal)	**61 16 8**

[1] sub-chapels, no full-time priest
[2] outlying farms belonging to the abbey and farmed by monks

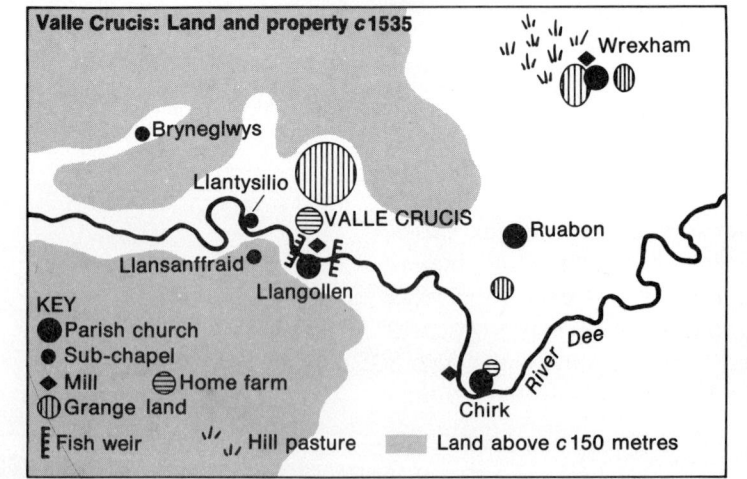

Valle Crucis: Land and property c1535

KEY
● Parish church
● Sub-chapel
◆ Mill   ⌂ Home farm
▥ Grange land
E Fish weir   Hill pasture   Land above c150 metres

	£ s d
Total abbey income	214 12 1
Regular out-payments (including alms)	26 4 1
Final abbey income	**188 8 0**

1 Imagine you are the cellarer, running the estate of Valle Crucis. Describe the problems you think this would involve. For example, how do you think they collected their tithes?

2 Look at the way 'spiritual income' was shared. How would this affect the four parishes?

3 Does it seem, from these figures, that Valle Crucis was spending a lot of money on alms?

The abbey at Valle Crucis suffered its misfortunes, like most other monastic houses. The number of monks was already dwindling when the Black Death, a terrible epidemic disease of the fourteenth century, killed about 25 per cent of the population of Europe. It weakened the monasteries very badly, and there were far fewer labouring monks to cultivate the huge estates of the Cistercians. After this time most of the abbey lands were rented out, and the abbots lived more and more like wealthy lords.

At Valle Crucis there was a devastating fire in the mid-thirteenth century, and at least one other late in the fourteenth or early fifteenth century. The second may have happened during the war of Owain Glyndŵr, the Welsh lord, who from 1400 to 1412 fought against the King for Wales's independence. This war caused enormous damage all over Wales: towns were burnt by Glyndŵr's men, while farms, crops, manor houses and villages were destroyed by the King's troops. The Cistercian monks supported Glyndŵr for the most part, and some were killed fighting with his forces. His efforts ended in defeat.

A pattern of leaves on a carved slab from Valle Crucis

Is this what Gutun Owain saw?

By the mid-fifteenth century the abbey had recovered well. Welsh poets described life there under a series of successful abbots. Both the following extracts are from poems dedicated to Dafydd ap Ieuan, abbot of Valle Crucis in the late fifteenth century, by travelling poets who found a warm welcome and good food whenever they visited the abbey:

> A golden haunt is the monastery,
> The choir *excels over* [is greater than] Salisbury,
> Its rich carvings,
> Leaves and statues
> And so many voices...
>
> His bright good house, a warm cloak,
> Its fine roof would *befit* [be suitable for] a fortress
> The sun's on the hill,
> And here's its house,
> Gleaming with whitewash,
> A glowing refuge.
>
> Gutun Owain, c1460–1500
>
> A good lord with many bells
> Maintains splendid *Glyn Egwestl* [the valley where Valle Crucis was built].
> The land's weak ones he cares for,
> A house he built across *Iâl* [the lordship where Glyn Egwestl lay],
> A web of stones his breastplate,
> Glass and lead's his mansion's base.
>
> Guto'r Glyn, c1450–90

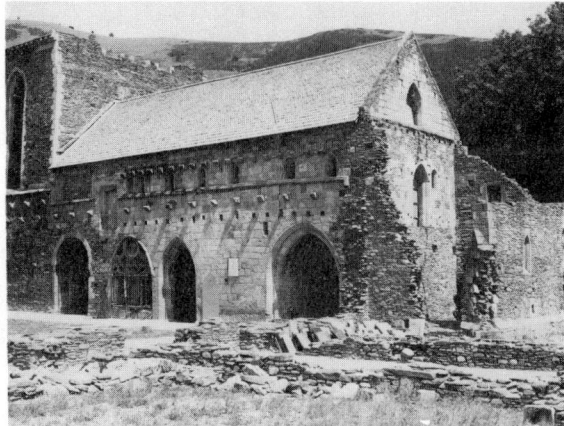

A modern view of the cloister at Valle Crucis, now in ruins, with part of the chapter house, where meetings were held, in the background

A drawing, made in 1913, of the east front of Valle Crucis, showing the part of the building that became a private house

It was enlarged after the monks' time.

One change in the later layout of the abbey buildings was the conversion of a large monks' dormitory, the 'dorter', into a separate abbot's house with its own front entrance. This shows how the abbot had become separated from the rest of the monks. In many places abbots were acting as justices of the peace – magistrates who held local courts. The abbots of thirty different houses were members of the House of Lords, like the bishops. But this last phase of glory for the monasteries was short-lived, as the next section will show.

1 Imagine you are the abbot of Valle Crucis, explaining to the monks in the chapter house your decision to restructure the dorter into an abbot's house with its own front door. How would you justify this?

2 The poets appreciated the abbeys' food and wine on their travels. Make a list of the other features they praise about Valle Crucis in the last two extracts. How many of these, do you think, really fit in with a monastery's religious purpose?

Changing attitudes

By the sixteenth century there had been many changes in the abbeys and nunneries of England and Wales. Even as far back as the twelfth century the monks had not been perfect. Gerald of Wales was an archdeacon in the Church and a well-informed and much-travelled writer. He compared some of the monastic orders in his own day:

people who give money; greed having one's own way; firmly

> In its original state of poverty the *Rule of Saint Benedict* was wholly admirable, but later on the order accumulated vast wealth through the fervent charity of great numbers of *benefactors* ... with the result that ... *gluttony* and *indulgence* ended in corruption. The Cistercian order ... clung *tenaciously* to its original vows of poverty and holiness ... but there again, ambition ... which sets no limit to our aspirations, crept up and took possession of it ...

> The Augustinian canons are more content than any of the others with a humble and modest mode of life... They dwell among *secular* [not connected with the Church] people, but they avoid as far as possible the temptations of this world.
>
> The Journey through Wales by Gerald of Wales, c1191

Comments were often made about the over-emphasis on worldly matters among the clergy. A thoughtful senior clergyman, John Colet, made this criticism in 1511:

> They [the clergy] give themselves to feasts and banqueting; they spend themselves in *vain babbling* [idle talk]; they give themselves to sports and plays; they apply themselves to hunting and hawking; they drown themselves in the delights of this world... For what other thing seek we nowadays in the Church than fat *benefices* [parish priests' posts] and high promotions? Yea, and in the same promotions, of what other things do we *pass upon* [talk about] than of our tithes and rents?
>
> A sermon by John Colet, Dean of St Paul's Cathedral, 1511

John Colet, 1467–1519

A biting criticism of the monks was published in 1528. It was a pamphlet by Simon Fish called *Supplication [Appeal] of the Beggars*. Fish, like most people, was a layman – a non-clergyman. His views may have reflected some of the strong feelings among lay people about the behaviour of monks and priests at the time:

> [The clergy]... have gotten into their hands more than the third part of all your realm. The goodliest lordships, manors, lands and territories are theirs. Besides this they have the tenth part of all the corn, meadow, pasture, grass, wool, colts, calves, lambs, pigs, geese and chickens. Over and besides, the tenth part of every servant's wages, the tenth part of the wool, milk, honey, wax, cheese and butter... What tyrant ever oppressed the people like this cruel and vengeful question?
>
> From *Supplication of the Beggars* by Simon Fish, 1528

Yet some monks still respected the *Rule*. In 1528 Cardinal Wolsey made Richard Bromeley, a monk of Valle Crucis, an exception to some parts of the Rule, excusing him from some of the harsher regulations of monastic life.

> Absolves him from the guilt... by the not wearing his habit... and gives him permission, because of his weakness of body, to use linen next the skin, and long leggings of a decent colour... under his *hood* [habit] during divine service... and to talk in a low voice in the dormitory and elsewhere... to eat and drink moderately.
>
> A permit from Cardinal Wolsey, 18 August 1528

A printing press at work in 1520

Printing enabled new ideas to spread quickly as books could be produced in large numbers.

What does Bromeley's application for such a permit reveal about Bromeley himself?

By the 1530s the abbeys of England and Wales had been caught up in the religious changes of King Henry VIII's reign. A quarrel had arisen between the King and the Pope over Henry's wish to divorce his queen and remarry. The Pope's refusal to allow the divorce angered Henry. He abolished the power of the Pope over the Church of England and made himself Head of the Church in his Kingdom.

The monasteries had been criticised often over the years, but the attacks became more serious in the 1530s. One reason for this was the new religious ideas which had been spreading all over Europe since the fifteenth century. Henry VIII's religious changes had introduced these ideas into England and Wales. The following documents offer some evidence which may help you to answer three important questions:

1. Did the new ideas change people's attitudes to the religious services provided by the monks?

bowing
making the sign of the cross

the perfection of Christian living doth not consist in dumb ceremonies, wearing of a grey coat, disguising ourselves after strange fashions, *ducking* and *becking*, in girding ourselves with a girdle full of knots, and other like papistical ceremonies, wherein we have been most principally practised and misled in times past.

Statement by the Grey Friars of Bedford, giving up their friary in 1538

helped; statues

[Nicholas Field] expounded to them many things... they that went on pilgrimage were accursed: that it *booted* not to pray to *images* for they were but stocks made of wood and could not help a man:

From *Actes and Monuments* by John Foxe, 1563

and though it be a good thing and much religious to pray for them which be departed out of this misery, yet we may not give all our possessions to nourish idle men in continual prayer for them, leaving others destitute of help which be in life.

A letter from Thomas Starkey to Henry VIII in 1536

2. Was the monastic way of life thought to be relevant to everyday life in England and Wales by the 1530s?

Religion is not contained in *apparel* [clothing], manner of going, shaven heads, and such other marks, nor in silence, fasting, uprising in the night, singing and other kind of ceremonies, but in cleanness of mind, pureness of living, Christ's faith not *feigned* [false] and brotherly charity.

From government rules issued to monasteries, 1535

The world in turmoil

A wood-carved cartoon of the 1500s shows the priest turned out to the plough and the peasant at the altar. What else is odd here?

The case of a monk seems to me to be different from that of a priest. The monk has voluntarily taken vows. You argue that a monastic vow is not binding because it is *incapable of fulfillment* [cannot be kept]... The real question is not whether vows can be kept, but whether they have been *enjoined* [ordered] by God.

I was a good monk and I kept the rule of my order... If I had kept on any longer, I should have killed myself with vigils, prayers, reading, and other work.

Good works do not make a man good, but a good man does good works.

Three comments by the religious reformer, Martin Luther (1483–1546)

3. How did the King and his ministers view the wealth and independence of the Church?

And what do all these greedy sort of sturdy, idle, holy thieves, with these yearly *exactions that they take of* [payments that they demand from] the people? Truly nothing but exempt themselves from the obedience of your *grace* [ie the King]. Nothing but translate all rule, power, lordship, authority, obedience and dignity from your grace unto them.

From *Supplication of the Beggars* by Simon Fish, 1528

This cartoon of the 1520s shows the quarrel between the Pope and different religious reformers in Europe.

it is well perceived by long approved experience that great and inestimable sums of money be daily conveyed out of this realm to the impoverishment of the same, and specially such sums... as the Pope's Holiness... by long time have *heretofore* taken.

From a law of Parliament stopping payments to the Pope, 1532

before this time

this realm of England is an Empire... governed by one supreme head and king... he being also institute and furnished... with... power... and jurisdiction to render and yield justice... to all manner of folk residents or subject within this his realm... without the intermeddling of any exterior person or persons.

From a law of Parliament banning legal appeals to the Pope, 1533

If it had been or were in my power to make you [the king] so rich as ye might enrich all men, God help me as I would do it.

Thomas Cromwell, the King's leading minister, just before his death in 1540

1 Which of the customs mentioned in the comments on page 20 were common practice in the monasteries? Which criticism, in your view, really struck at the heart of the purpose of the monasteries?

2 Was Martin Luther arguing that (a) being a monk was too difficult, or (b) that there was no real purpose to monastic life?

3 The extracts above could be used as evidence to back up these four statements. Match each statement to the extract which supports it.
(a) The Pope was taking money out of the kingdom.
(b) The clergy were putting themselves above the King's laws.
(c) The King needed more money.
(d) The King claimed the right to rule everyone in the land.

The storm breaks

Carthusian monks being hanged, disembowelled and quartered

Ten of them suffered this fate between 1535 and 1540. This picture was drawn in Rome many years later.

The picture above shows monks of the Carthusian order being hanged in 1535. They had refused to accept Henry VIII's claim to be head of the Church. Elizabeth Barton, a Benedictine nun from Kent, had been executed in 1534. They were all treated as traitors for opposing the King's religious changes and refusing to accept Henry as head of the Church. Some reformers wanted still more changes, while many people looked longingly at the Church's great wealth.

These dramatic changes were not the only problems facing the small abbey of Valle Crucis in the 1530s. Like many other monasteries, looking after its property had become an all-important matter. Many abbots looked on abbey wealth as their personal, or family, property. Sometimes son followed father as abbot, as in Basingwerk Abbey, a few miles from Valle Crucis. This happened in spite of the fact that monks were not supposed to marry or have children. Robert Salusbury, abbot of Valle Crucis, dragged his abbey into the quarrels and feuds that raged between the landowning families of North Wales.

Robert Salusbury was related to a powerful family of the same name with its home at Lleweni, near Denbigh in Clwyd. His family's influence probably helped him to become abbot, but soon after his appointment he was in conflict with another Welsh clergyman who also belonged to a landowning family and had strong ambitions. This man, Robert ap Rhys, was a priest working for Cardinal Wolsey, the King's leading minister until 1529. Ap Rhys used his position to build up a profitable estate in his home district. He and his brothers clashed with the Salusburys in the process. Robert ap Rhys also used his Church and government contacts to make life difficult for Abbot Salusbury at Valle Crucis. He brought criminal charges against the abbot in the early 1530s. The chain of investigation and scandal that followed ended in Robert Salusbury's imprisonment in the Tower of London and shattered morale at the abbey.

Robert ap Rhys charged Salusbury and his brothers with forcing their way on to his property and seizing land of his in three counties. The abbot retaliated by charging ap Rhys's son with assault and stealing some of his possessions at Wrexham. But more serious trouble was brewing for Salusbury.

The jig-saw pieces of the scandal at Valle Crucis have to be pieced together from official letters and papers kept at the time. Two of them were written to William Brereton, a Cheshire squire, who was executed in 1536. Lists of his land and income made after his death may show why events in North Wales were of interest to him, and to the Duke of Richmond, who ordered an investigation at Valle Crucis.

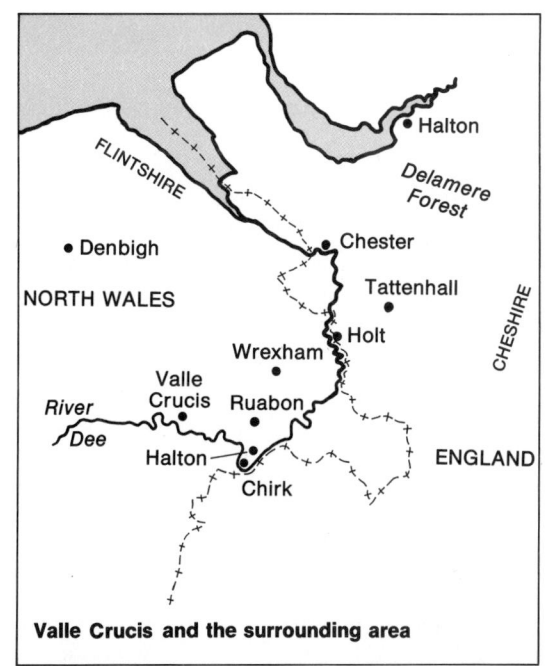

Valle Crucis and the surrounding area

Lands in farm of the King:—To him and my lady in survivorship, lordship of Echells, 68*l.* 6*s.* 3½*d.*, manor of Alderlaie, 20*l.* 12*s.* 5½*d.*, and manor and lordship of Aldeford, Chesh., 53*l.* 14*s.* 1½*d.*, with lands of Aldeforde, in Flintshire, 106*s.* 8*d.*; in all 47*l.* clear, and the King paid. Lordship of Mottrom in Londendale, 46*l.* 19*s.* 2*d.*, to him and his brother Uryan in survivorship, manor and lordship of Shotwyks and Sage Hall, 22*l.* 12*s.* 8*d.*; lands in Chester, parcel of Mottrom in Longdendale, 20*s.*, to him and his heirs; manor of Lesnes, ——;* lands in Charleyton, Chesh., 6*l.* 14*s.* 8*d.*; ferries of North Wales, 20*l.* 2*s.* 4*d.* clear; lordship of Fyncheley, Midd., 25*l.* 19*s.* 4½*d.*: total 271*l.* 7*s.* 9*d.* Lands in farm of the duke of Richmond:—Demesnes of Holt Castle, with the "weyre houks" and other pasture in the lordship of Bromefeld, 19*l.* 17*s.* 9*d.*; the horsemill in Holt town, 33*s.* 4*d.*: total, 21*l.* 11*s.* 1*d.*

In farm:—of Dr. Chamber, tithe corn of Pykyll, 13*l.* 6*s.* 8*d.*; of the abbot of Vala Crucis, tithe corn of Ruabon, 26*l.* 13*s.* 4*d.*, "for the which he paid nothing:" total, 40*l.* Offices by the King:—chamberlainship of Chester, 22*l.* 10*s.*, and Randall Brereton for the fee of chamberlain, 26*l.* 13*s.* 4*d.*, 49*l.* 3*s.* 4*d.* clear; constable of Chester castle, 18*l.* 5*s.*; escheator of Chester, 10*l.* 10*s.*; rangership of Dalamer forest, 4*l.* 11*s.* 3*d.*; stewardship of Halton, 100 [*s.*]; comptrollership of Chester and Flintshire, 12*l.* 3*s.* 4*d.*; stewardship of Bromefeld, 20*l.*; receivership there, 13*l.* 6*s.* 8*d.*; master fostership, 60*s.*; office of serjeant at Paxe there, 4*l.*; of improver there, 60*s.* 10*d.*; keeping of Mersley park, 60*s.* 10*d.*; stewardship of Crykeland, 10*l.*; receivership there, 100*s.*; annuity of Denbigh, 6*l.* 13*s.* 4*d.*; sheriffship of Flintshire, 20*l.*; keeping of Halton park, 60*s.* 10*d.*: total, 190*l.* 15*s.* 5*d.*

Extracts from 'Letters and Papers . . . of the Reign of Henry VIII': summaries of old official papers printed in 22 volumes between 1862 and 1932

The investigation was carried out by one of the three official inspectors of Cistercian abbeys. This was none other than Leyshon Thomas, abbot of Neath (see page 3). He wrote on 17 February 1535:

> I have been at . . . Valle Crucis . . . and did accuse the abbot their master of divers crimes and excesses . . . On the morrow after being *co-assistant* with the abbots of Conwy, Cymer and of Cwmhir, the abbot . . . brought forth certain *exceptions* against the prior and 2 others that they were informers and polluted with divers crimes . . . so that by law they were not able to accuse him, but I would not accept such exceptions *of* him. Wherewith he and his learned counsel was sore grieved.

in consultation with

objections

from

A monk and a nun being punished publicly in the stocks

1 There is a serious weakness in this report as evidence of the 'scandal' at Valle Crucis. What is it?

2 Does Abbot Salusbury seem to have been prepared to take responsibility for his alleged 'crimes and excesses'?

What were Salusbury's crimes? We have to look elsewhere for those details, and historians have found them among the government papers of Thomas Cromwell. The scene moves to Oxford where a goldsmith called Robert Hall had been sent to Oxford gaol for forgery. This next letter was written to Cromwell by Sir Walter Stonor, an Oxfordshire magistrate, probably in May 1535:

> He [Hall] stated that if I would be his good master he would betray a great nest of thieves. As I could not go myself I wrote to the said Hall [asking him] to tell me his secrets, and if I found it to be true I would befriend him. I sent his letter here inclosed. On receipt of it I sent to Oxford to take the said abbot and others specified in it, who had fled to London, where Hall was taken. Since then it is said that £140 have been found with him. The abbot is abbot of Valle Crucis, in Wales, and is a White Monk, named Salusbury. If it be your pleasure, I will speak to Hall, because my neighbour Hamylden was robbed on Shrove Sunday last, when the said abbot and William Pigott and Jones mentioned in the letter were present. They have committed many robberies, as Hall says.
>
> Letter from Sir Walter Stonor to Thomas Cromwell, May 1535

3 Imagine yourself as a detective sifting through the contents of Stonor's letter, before talking to Hall, and list the points in it that could be used as evidence.

This is the letter from Robert Hall that Stonor sent on to Cromwell:

> This is the truth of the robbery of Hamlynton. The thieves were, my lord Abbot named Salusbury, William Pigott, his servant, Master Jones, James Whelar, Perys Felde and Robert Hall, goldsmith.

> The Abbot is at the White Friars of Oxford, or else at the Bells, Kedlenton... You shall know more when I speak with you. Jones and *the other* met at the White Friars gate in Oxford, at the next house to the gate towards the town. Whatever they took, the Abbot and Master Jones had all, and none of us had one penny.

Abbot Salusbury

1 The 'White Friars of Oxford' meant the Carmelite Friary in Oxford, but what kind of place was 'the Bells, Kedlenton'?

2 Why do you think Hall was giving away all this information?

3 Can you think of any points *for* and any points *against* his reliability as a witness?

So Robert Salusbury was a bandit – not a common pastime for an abbot. He was arrested soon after, and was in the Tower of London for a time, as the following record shows:

> In the White Tower, Robert Salusbury, of the abbey of Valle Crucis, Roger Sparke, of the Nantwich, Robert Hall of Oxfordshire, goldsmith, Steven Sumner, smith, of Tarporley, Cheshire, John Wryce, smith, of Nantwich, Thomas Cotgreve, of Barrow, Ph. Constantine, of Chester.
>
> From a government list of prisoners in the Tower of London, *c*July 1535

Abbot Salusbury was to make one more appearance in the story of Valle Crucis, as we shall see later on this chapter. But the fate of his small abbey was now closely linked with that of 847 other houses of its kind.

A highway robbery in the sixteenth century

What did the King mean to do?

Thomas Cromwell, 1485–1540, a blacksmith's son who became Henry VIII's most powerful minister

Henry VIII's council
It included lords, bishops and professionals like Cromwell.

Henry VIII's ministers and many powerful people up and down the land were hostile to the monasteries by 1535. But what did the King and his government mean to do about them? Did they mean to close them all down or to tighten up their discipline? There are some clues, but no firm answers, to be found in the documents that survive from that era. A law made in 1534 had given the King the following powers over the Church:

> our said sovereign lord the King ... shall have full power and authority from time to time to visit, repress, redress, reform, order, correct, restrain and amend all such errors, heresies, abuses, offences, contempts and enormities, whatsoever they be.
>
> The Act of Supremacy, 1534

■ Check the meanings of the words from the Act of Supremacy, using a dictionary. Make sure you can explain the difference between 'repress' and 'redress', which look very similar. Would you call the King's new powers 'wide-ranging' or 'limited'?

Thomas Cromwell, the King's chief minister, could use this power on the King's behalf. He made new sets of rules for the monasteries in 1535. These were issued to the monks by a team of monastery inspectors along with instructions to obey them in future.

Here are some of the rules sent out to monasteries:

> that no monk or brother of this monastery by any means go *forth of the precincts of the same*.
>
> leave the monastery grounds
>
> Also that women ... be utterly excluded from entering ... this monastery or place unless they first obtain *licence* ...
>
> permission
>
> Also that all ... brethren and monks ... take their *refections* all together ... not ... *demanding to them* any ... portion of meat, as they were wont to do, but that they be content with such *victual* as is set before them, and there take their refection soberly without excess, giving due thanks to God;
>
> meals
> asking for food
>
> From the King's Injunctions for Monasteries, 1535

■ Do the rules quoted above look like an effort (a) to close down the monasteries, or (b) to improve their standards?

One very firm opinion was given in this next document, written in 1534 by a government official whose name is unrecorded:

> that the king's highness may have ... for the maintenance of his royal estate and ... to use and *disburse* for the defence of the realm all the lands and possessions of monasteries, abbeys, priories, and houses of religion ... whereof the number in any one house is or of late hath been ... under 13 persons.
>
> spend
>
> From an anonymous manuscript in the British Library

1 How does the above statement compare with the law of 1534 authorising the king to 'reform, order, correct ... and amend'?

2 How would the anonymous author spend the money that was gained by the government?

Mealtime at a Cistercian abbey in Italy

A modern photograph of a former abbey dining hall in Canterbury

27

Charles, King of Spain and Holy Roman Emperor, was told about Henry VIII's religious changes by his ambassador in London, Eustace Chapuys.

A few other remarks made by people close to the centres of power may help us to decide what the government really intended. This comment was made by John Price, one of the official investigators, in a report that a number of nuns had been begging in tears to be dismissed from their convent because they could not accept the new rules:

> They will all do this [leave the abbey] if they are compelled to observe these instructions.
>
> John Price, 1535

This is what the Spanish Ambassador to London had written to the King of Spain about Henry VIII's religious changes in 1534, though you should bear in mind that he may have been angry as a result of Henry's divorce from Catherine of Aragon, who was Spanish:

small income

obtain money from

> The king, who, as head of the Church in his kingdom, was intending to take back into his hands all church property and distribute only a *frugal sustenance* to ministers of the Church, is for the present satisfied to leave the churchmen in possession of their property, provided they will contribute ... Since the king was determined to *bleed* the churchmen he has done much better to do it thus than to take all their goods, to avoid the murmur and hatred, not only of the clergy but of the people.
>
> Report by Spanish ambassador, Eustace Chapuys, to Emperor Charles V, 28 November, 1534

The two comments below are attributed to Thomas Cromwell. He was the man at the head of the government during the closing of the monasteries, so his views are important. Here, we see two different ways in which historical evidence can survive. He made the first comment in writing, in notes about the state of the monasteries, dated February 1536. These notes still exist, so we can be sure of their accuracy.

rottenness; improvement planned out

> the *abomination* of religious persons throughout this realm and a *reformation* to be *devised therein*.
>
> Notes by Thomas Cromwell, February 1536

This second comment is *said* to have been made by Cromwell at a meeting of the King's Council in 1536. It appears in a chronicle, a kind of historical diary, written many years later, and was found among the papers of a seventeenth-century civil servant, George Wyatt:

even though it was done gently

> For when the late Cardinal Wolsey had obtained your Majesty's favour ... to dissolve certain monasteries ... yet the same (*were it never so gently done* ... and that by one and one) was not done without some Disquiet, as everybody knoweth. Wherefore mine advice is that it should be done by little and little not suddenly by parliament.
>
> From *A Chronicle and Defence of the English Reformation*, written after 1600 (author unknown)

This comment was recorded through hearsay so we cannot be sure how accurate it really is.

Have the extracts you have been reading helped you to judge what the government planned to do? How useful and dependable are they? The following table should help you to sort out the different extracts and give your verdict on each one.

Make your own copy of the table below and give points in each category to each of the seven extracts. Award the points on a scale from 0 to 4: 4 for a high rating, 0 for the bottom rating. Add up the total for each extract and see how each one rates.

Henry VIII, c1540

He was ruthless in demanding his own way, and he used men like Cromwell to achieve it.

	Closeness in time to the event	Author directly involved	Author well-placed for news	Balanced, fair account	Clear in meaning	**Total**
1. Act of Supremacy, 1534						
2. Injunctions to Monasteries, 1535						
3. Anonymous plan, 1534						
4. John Price's comment, 1535						
5. Ambassador Chapuys, 1534						
6. Cromwell's note, 1536						
7. *A Chronicle and Defence* after 1600						

Now that you have studied the evidence, you can make your own judgement about what was intended. A summary of possible choices is shown on the next page, but you may choose a different solution if you wish.

Make a copy of this table and give each possible intention a grade (A, B, C etc). The one you think is most likely will be 'A', the next will be 'B' and so on. If you write in a suggestion of your own, give that a grade too.

Intention	
1. Quick, total closure of all religious houses	
2. Improved discipline in all religious houses	
3. Closure of small houses and raised standards in the others	
4. Gradual, 'softly-softly' closure of all houses	
5.	

Steps to closure

In just two years the government took a series of five 'steps' which ended up with the closure of the monasteries.

Step 1 The *Valor Ecclesiasticus*
Parliament had made a law in 1534 demanding taxes from all the clergy. But to get its money the government had to find out just how much income the churches, monasteries and other houses were taking in. So committees were set up all over the kingdom to make lists of all Church property and its current value. These detailed lists were gathered together in London, and are known as the *Valor Ecclesiasticus* (Church Valuation). The survey began in January 1535 but it was not completed until the following winter. By that time a different team of people was going around the countryside acting on Cromwell's 'Step 3'.

Step 2 The Vicar-General
Thomas Cromwell was made Vicar-General of the Church of England by the King on 21 January 1535. This gave him power over the entire Church organisation. Now he could order a general 'visitation', or inspection, of all religious houses and their activities.

Step 3 The *Compendium Compertorum* (Collection of Facts)
This report was prepared by a team of investigators appointed by Cromwell in the summer of 1535 to collect as much information as possible on all monasteries and nunneries. There were four leading investigators: Richard Layton, Thomas Legh, John Price and John Tregonwell. Layton, Legh and Price spent the summer and autumn touring the monasteries and nunneries

of southern England, except for a visit to Leeds by Layton. Tregonwell concentrated on the Midlands and the west of England.

Three other officials, Adam Becanshaw, John Vaughan and Elis Prys visited houses in Wales. Prys was dismissed, however, after the other two had complained to Cromwell about his behaviour. He took a girl with him around the monasteries and:

> showed in taverns the King's Commission to advance himself, which causeth the people to murmur. He does not regard my admonition to leave such young touches.
>
> Letter by Becanshaw to Cromwell

■ Why do you think these complaints about Prys made Cromwell decide to dismiss him?

A modern painting of commissioners visiting an abbey

Does the artist give any hint of the attitude of the commissioners or the abbot?

Step 3 ended after Layton and Legh had made a huge sweep across northern England in the winter of 1535-6, visiting 121 religious houses in two months. Other investigators, including John London, Thomas Bedyll and Richard Pollard worked on later surveys when the larger abbeys were being closed down.

What were the investigators looking for? They were given a set of questions to be asked and topics to be looked into. Some of these are shown in the next extract:

> 1 Whether divine service is duly observed. 2 How many inmates there are or ought to be ... 15-23 The rule of the house and how it is observed and whether any women are lodged in the precincts. 24-7 How far the articles specified in their rule are kept.... 76-86 Conversation and behaviour of the nuns, and how often they confess.
>
> Articles for the visitation of the monasteries, January 1535

The investigators also took with them the strict new rules that were now to be enforced. You have seen extracts from them on page 27. Each investigator was given a 'commission', or a licence proving his authority. Among other things, the investigators had to check:

> the lives and morals of their abbots, removing and punishing those whom they find at fault, and receiving resignations of those willing to resign, giving them pensions, and appointing their successors.
>
> Investigator's Royal Commission, 1535

The powers granted to the investigators were very useful in monasteries where there were problems, such as Valle Crucis.

We know that Abbot Salusbury of Valle Crucis was in serious trouble in May 1535 and was in the Tower of London by July. In August he made what must have been his last appearance at Valle Crucis, when the investigators Becanshaw and Vaughan visited the abbey:

Inside the chapter house at Valle Crucis

The commissioners may have met the monks here in September 1535.

> From the 22nd to the 26th August we visited the abbey of Valle Crucis, where many things require reformation. The abbot came in, *was sworn* [took an oath] and examined, and carried by Mr. Brereton's servants to the castle of Holt, and one of his monks, whom we took, being *apostata* [guilty of a serious breach of his vows], where they await the King's pleasure. The monastery and the church are in great decay, and indebted to the King and others 300 marks [£200]. We intend to *deprive the abbot* [dismiss him officially] on the 4th or 5th Sept., and wish to know your pleasure for a new election. There are six monks in the house, but none fit for abbot except the prior, a good, virtuous and well-disposed man; but abbot there he will not be in no case, as he saith, considering the said house to be already so far in debt and decay, whereby it is not like whosoever shall have the same that ever he shall do any good upon it. The abbot of Cymer [near Dolgellau, Gwynedd] who is a *good husband* [efficient manager], would *fain* [gladly] have it, and would give you £20 towards your duty, but no more.
>
> Report by Becanshaw and Vaughan to Cromwell, 1 September 1535

■ In which ways were the special powers of the investigators effective at Valle Crucis?

Step 4 The First Act for the Dissolution (closure) of the Monasteries, 1536. In the spring of 1536 Members of Parliament were summoned to London to vote on a new law concerning the monasteries. This law, or 'act', closed down all the smaller religious houses – those with an income of less than £200 a year. A paragraph at the beginning of the Act explained why this was done. Here is an extract from it:

> sin, vicious, carnal and abominable living, is daily used and committed amongst the little and small ... religious houses of monks, canons and nuns, where the congregation ... is under the number of twelve persons, whereby the governors of such religious houses and their convent, spoil, destroy, consume, and utterly waste, as well their churches, [and] monasteries, ... farms, granges, lands ... such small houses [should] be utterly suppressed and the religious persons therein committed to great and honourable monasteries ... where they may be compelled to live religiously for *reformation* of their lives.

improvement

Act for the Dissolution of the Monasteries, 1536

■ Did the makers of this law see any difference between the standard of monastic life in the bigger monasteries and in the smaller ones?

An abbey barn at Glastonbury, Somerset

Farm produce paid as tithe would be stored here for the abbey's use.

Step 5 The Suppression Commissioners
As a result of the law passed in Step 4, commissioners were appointed again to visit the smaller abbeys and close them down. They were not simply investigating now, but carrying out very definite and drastic orders. The questionnaires they took with them asked for the following details:

> 1. Name [of abbey], religion, *to whom they be cells*, and value at the last valuation. 2. Clear yearly value at this new survey. 3. Number of religious persons, with their lives, *conversations*, how many are priests, and how many will

which was their mother-monastery, as Strata Marcella was to Valle Crucis

conduct

licences to become parish priests; farm-workers

will have *capacities*. 4. Number of servants, *hinds*, and other persons having the living of the house. 5. Value of bells, lead, and other buildings to be sold, with the estate or ruin of the house. 6. Entire value of moveable goods, stocks and stores, with debts owing to the house. 7. The woods, with the age of them, parks, forests, and commons, belonging to the house, and number of acres.

priories or small monastic cells, which were

8. Debts owing to the house. 9. The *houses of religion, and* left out at the last valuation.

1 Do these questions suggest to you what the government meant to do with the monastic houses that they closed?

2 To what use would an abbey put its 'parks, forests, and commons'?

3 Why should the commissioners want to know the age of the abbey woods?

The final days of Valle Crucis, 1536

The ruined church at Valle Crucis today

Anne Boleyn, Henry VIII's queen from 1533 to 1536

Valle Crucis was one of those smaller abbeys closed under the 1536 Act. At the time of the 1535 survey the abbey's property was worth a total of £214 12s 1d; but the regular payments the abbey had to make brought its real income down to £188 8s. This meant that Valle Crucis was below the vital £200 level. One of the priorities of the officials who came to close it was to order the head of a doomed house not to spend any money or collect rents, since all abbey property was now the King's. As we saw on page 23, one abbot, Salusbury, had only just been dismissed from Valle Crucis. In those last months of the abbey's life, the abbot's job was given as a 'reward' to a London monk who had friends in senior government positions. Similar arrangements were made in other houses to give favoured people a few months' income and the chance of a pension after closure. This next letter gives some clues to what was happening, and to an unexpected link between Valle Crucis and the tragic fate of Queen Anne Boleyn who was beheaded in 1536 by order of her husband, Henry VIII. The exercise on page 36 will help you find out more about this.

> I have been with my lord of Rochford ... he says that he *made suit* to you for promotion of a White Monk, of the Tower Hill, and with your help he was promoted to the abbey of Vale Sante Crewsys, in Cheshire, and *he had for his promotion £100* ... He supposes the said abbey is *suppressed* and the abbot *undone*,
>
> Letter from Sir William Kingston to Thomas Cromwell, 18 May 1536

applied

he accepted a bribe of £100; closed
dismissed

A nineteenth-century picture of Anne Boleyn's execution in May 1536

No record exists of the actual closure of Valle Crucis Abbey, but it must have occurred some time during that summer of 1536. Records do show that the abbey estates were in private hands by 1537. Abbot John was granted a pension of £23 a year after the Dissolution, but the remaining monks were given only £10 13s 4d a year between them. It is not known whether all the six who had been there in 1535 got pensions: if so they were probably very poor ones.

An Exercise in Historical Research

Can you find out who Lord Rochford and Sir William Kingston were?

The best place to look for details about a character from British history is in a set of bulky volumes called the *Dictionary of National Biography*. There is usually a set to be found in public libraries, and often in school libraries too. Unfortunately, Sir William Kingston does not appear in it, and Lord Rochford is not there under that name. So where do we go next? The year 1536 was during the reign of King Henry VIII. There is a very good book about his long reign by J J Scarisbrick, entitled *Henry VIII*. The index at the back lists all the important people mentioned in the book. Under 'Rochford' it says 'see Boleyn, Thomas and George'. You can look up these two men on the pages listed after their names, or you can now look up 'Boleyn' in the *Dictionary of National Biography* or an encyclopaedia such as *Encyclopaedia Britannica* or *Chambers' Encyclopaedia*.

You will have seen by now that Lord Rochford was, in fact, George Boleyn, brother of Henry VIII's divorced queen, Anne Boleyn, and that he was executed within days of his sister, in May 1536! But what about Sir William Kingston? Details of him can be found in *The Lisle Letters*; these are a collection of letters written in Henry VIII's time. The index to the published letters gives the following details about Kingston:

KINGSTON (Kyngston; Kyngeston), Sir William, captain of the Guard 1523–39, constable of the Tower 1524–40, Vice-Chamberlain 1536–9,

From *The Lisle Letters* edited by Muriel St Clare Byrne, 1981

What can you piece together from these bits of information? It seems that Kingston was in command of the Tower of London at the time of the imprisonment and execution of Anne Boleyn and her brother, Lord Rochford, in May 1536. The Boleyn family were victims of Henry VIII's anger, and their fate had no direct link with the closing of the abbeys. Rochford, however, tried to persuade his gaoler to do him a favour during his last days. He probably asked Kingston to secure further help, perhaps a pension, for the 'White Monk' who had paid Rochford £100. This monk, the last abbot of Valle Crucis, was a Cistercian monk of St Mary Graces Abbey, on Tower Hill, London. His first name was John, but records of his surname vary between Heron, Herne and Deram.

The Tower of London in 1547

It was used as a prison for important victims of the King's anger, like Anne Boleyn, Rochford and Brereton, as well as criminals like Hall and Salusbury.

The 1536 Dissolution closed down a total of 243 religious houses – no more than 30 per cent of the total number in England and Wales. None of the 187 houses of friars was affected at all, and another 176 houses were allowed to continue even though their incomes were below £200 a year. The really dramatic changes, which left not a single monastery or nunnery open, were yet to come. This is how one of the Crown's own commissioners appealed for a reprieve for a small nunnery in Warwickshire in 1536:

> we have surveyed the monastery or nunnery of Pollesworth in the county of Warwick, wherein is an abbess named dame Alice Fitzherbert, of the age of 60 years, a very sad, discreet, and religious woman, and hath been head and governor there 27 years, and in the same house under her rule are 12 virtuous and religious nuns, and of good *conversation* as far as we can hear or perceive, as well by our examinations as by the *open fame* and report of all the country, and never one of the nuns there will leave nor forsake their habit and religion. Wherefore . . . ye might do a right good and meritorious deed to be a *mediator* to the King's highness for the said house to stand and remain *unsuppressed*, for, as we think, ye shall not speak in the *preferment* of a better nunnery nor of better women. And in the town of Pollesworth are 44 *tenements*, and never a plough but one, the residue be *artificers*, labourers, and *victuallers*, and live in effect by the said house.
>
> Report by the commissioners to Cromwell, 28 July 1536

conversation — conduct
open fame — public reputation
mediator — speaker on behalf of
open
preferment — favour
tenements — plots rented out
artificers; victuallers — craftsmen; dealers in food and drink

■ How many reasons are given in the last extract for not suppressing Pollesworth nunnery?

At Valle Crucis there was no reprieve. The last exit of the monks may have been like the scene at Roche Abbey, another Cistercian house, which is described on the next page.

This description of the closure of the Yorkshire abbey of Roche, closed in 1538, was written by a local man in 1591:

> the Visitors should come suddenly upon every house and unawares ... to take them napping ... least if they should have had so much as any inkling of their coming, they would have made conveyance of some part of their own goods to help themselves ... for so soon as the Visitors were entered within the gates, they called the Abbot and other Officers of the House, and caused them to deliver up to them all their keys and took an *inventory* of all their goods, both within doors and *without* ... and when they had so done, turned the Abbot with all his convent and household forth of the doors.
>
> Which thing was not a little grief to the Convent, and all the Servants of the House departing one from another ... for it would have made an heart of flint to have melted and wept to have seen the breaking up of the house, and their sorrowful departure; and the sudden *spoil* that fell the same day of their departure from the House.
>
> From an anonymous manuscript in the British Library, written *c*1591

list
outside

looting

1 Which of these *adjectives* (describing words) is the best to describe the attitude of the author whose words you have just read: (a) uncaring, (b) cruel, (c) sorrowful, (d) glad?

2 Would you say that this account is what a modern newsman might call an 'immediate, up-to-the-minute report' of what happened at Roche? Rewrite the account, as though you were a journalist writing for your local newspaper, or draw a picture to show the events that took place at Roche.

3 Imagine you are meeting a relative, in 1536, who has been abroad and out of touch with the news for some three years. Write a short explanation of the changes in religion and the Church that have taken place in England and Wales during that time.

The ruins of Roche Abbey, in Yorkshire

'Bare walls standing'

A German cartoon from the sixteenth century showing church statues and ornaments being smashed as a religious protest

Stepping up the pressure

The campaign against the monasteries was far from over. Indeed the government propaganda was stepped up from 1536 onwards. The government launched an official campaign against praying in front of saints' relics and images (religious paintings and statues), which is yet another example of their all-out attack on the monasteries. The monasteries had for centuries been important centres for **pilgrims**. These were people who travelled long distances to pray at sites connected with great religious figures from the past. They believed that the effort and the prayers they made could bring the spirit of a dead saint to intercede or speak on their behalf to God. Most of the important shrines were either in monasteries or run by the monks. The donations of pilgrims were a good source of income for the monks. The reports of 1536 and later brought in plenty of evidence about relics and images as the following extracts show:

> Amongst the relics we found much vanity and superstition, as the coals that Saint Laurence was toasted with, the pareing of St Edmund's nails, St Thomas of Canterbury's penknife and his boots, and divers *skulls for the headache*; pieces of the holy cross able to make a whole cross.
>
> Letter by John Price to Cromwell from Bury St Edmunds, 5 November 1535

saints' relics used as healing charms

> within the said diocese of St Asaph... there is an image of Derfel Gadarn ... in whom the people have so great confidence, hope and trust, that they come daily a pilgrimage unto him, some with cattle, others with oxen or horses, and the rest with money, insomuch that there was five or six hundred pilgrims to *a man's estimation* [at a guess] that *offered* [made offerings] to the said image the fifth day of this present month of April... there is a common saying... that whosoever will offer any thing to the said image of Derfel Gadarn, he hath power to fetch him... out of hell when they be damned.
>
> Letter from Elis Prys, a monastery inspector, to Cromwell, 6 April 1538

Carved figures of monks praying, from Italy

The Pilgrimage of Grace, 1536-7

This event was not really a pilgrimage, but a rebellion. Trouble began with an uprising in Lincolnshire in October 1536 which soon spread to northern England. By early 1537 seven northern counties were affected, especially Yorkshire and Lancashire. It was led by a group of lords, country squires and clergy, but large numbers of poor people joined the revolts too. There were many reasons for it, such as interference by government officials in local affairs and heavy taxes. But most of all the rebels disliked the changes in religion. Robert Aske, one of the leaders of the rebellion, made this the first of five complaints:

closure

without relief, i.e. in times of distress

nuns

The *suppression* of so many religious houses as are at this instant time suppressed, whereby the service of our God is not well maintained but also the commons of your realm be *unrelieved*, the which we think is a great hurt to the common wealth and many *sisters* be put from their livings and left at large.

From Aske's list of complaints at York, 15 October 1536

These lines come from two ballads of the time. One may have been the work of Cistercian monks from Sawley Abbey, Lancashire, which had just been closed down. The author of the second is unknown:

The Pilgrimage of Grace as a nineteenth-century artist saw it. The banners show the wounds of Christ.

Great God's fame
Doth Church proclaim
Now to be lame
And *fast in bounds* [tied down],
Robbed, spoiled and shorn
From cattle and corn,
And *clean forth borne*
Of [deprived of] houses and lands.
Alack! Alack!
For the church's sake
Poor commons wake,
And no marvel!
For clear it is
How the poor shall miss
No tongue can tell.
For there they had
Both ale and bread
At time of need,
And *succour* [help] great
In all distress
And heaviness
And *well entreat* [were well treated].

Pilgrims Ballad, 1536

Abbeys to suppress we have little need,
The which *of* [from] charity good men did
    found;
To them it was thought it was great-made;
But boldly now down straight to the ground
Many are busy them to decay,
And them *profaneth* [make them unsacred]:
    none dare say nay.

An Exhortation to the North, 1536

The ruined infirmary, or hospital, of Furness Abbey

Sick monks went there for treatment, and elderly monks retired there to end their days, before the Dissolution.

1 What particular things did the writers of these ballads miss about the abbeys, and what did they dislike about their fate?

The revolt was finally crushed early in 1537 and its leaders were executed, including Robert Aske. Among the monks involved were 32 Cistercians from Furness Abbey. A friar who was at Furness at the time gave this information under interrogation:

> I have heard the bailiff of Dalton say the monks encouraged the commons, saying: 'Now must they stick to it or else never, for if they sit down both you and Holy Church is undone; and if they lack company we will go with them and live and die with them to defend their most godly pilgrimage.' The prior and brethren gave them £20...
>
> *Salley* had said it was never a good world since 'secular men and knaves had rule upon us and the King made head of the Church'.
>
> Friar Dalton's evidence

a monk

The heads of two Lincolnshire monasteries and of six in northern England were executed for treason, along with many ordinary monks. Their involvement with rebels was the cause. Some of their monasteries, like Sawley, had already been closed officially in 1536. Now the King closed all the 'rebel' abbeys.

2 Why are ballads like the two you have seen, useful to historians? What sort of information do they provide?

3 There were a number of ballads sung about the rebellions of 1536. Why do you think they were so popular?

4 Write a short ballad or poem of your own, with a rhyme every other line if you can find one! Describe in your ballad any important news event of today. Suppose you are a historian, centuries from now: how much information could he get from your ballad about that event, if no other record of it had survived? Would it make sense?

The abbeys surrender

The climate of fear created by Henry VIII's ruthless policies made the abbots of the large monasteries anxious. Thomas Cromwell had prepared the ground for his next step very carefully, according to an anonymous writer from the time of Elizabeth I, many years later:

He placed abbots and friars in divers great houses, divers learned men, and persuaded against superstitions, *which* men were ready to make surrender of their houses at the King's commandment.

From *The Manner of Dissolving the Abbeys by King Henry VIII*, an anonymous sixteenth-century manuscript in the British Library

these (gloss for *which*)

Cromwell now began to use the bullying tactics of his commissioners plus the promise of good pensions for the abbots, to persuade them all to 'surrender' their houses. An abbot and his 'chapter' (abbey management committee) would be persuaded to hand over the abbey and all its property to the King. They were also told that all Church property now belonged to the King anyway. The abbot and the other monks would then be offered pensions or appointed as clergymen to nearby churches. The first surrender of this sort came in April 1537: Furness Abbey, rocked to its foundations by the arrests after the Pilgrimage of Grace, handed itself over to the King on 5 April.

Later the same year, the great abbey of Lewes, in Sussex, was handed over in the same way. This opened a floodgate of similar surrenders which went on until 1540, when Waltham Abbey, London, closed its doors on 23 March. King Henry's hatchet men did not frighten everyone. Commissioner John London found Abbess Katherine Bulkeley of Godstow, near Oxford, a determined woman:

doctor John London, which, as your lordship doth well know, was against my promotion, and hath ever since borne me great malice and grudge, like my mortal enemy, is suddenly come unto me with a great *rout* with him, and here doth threaten me and my sisters, saying that he hath the king's *commission* to suppress the house *spite of my teeth*. And when he saw that ... I would never surrender to his hand, being my ancient enemy, now he begins to entreat me and to *inveigle* my sisters one by one.

Abbess Katherine Bulkeley's letter to Cromwell, November 1538

- *rout* — group of followers
- *commission* — authority
- *spite of my teeth* — in spite of my objections
- *inveigle* — persuade

The Abbess got her way. Godstow was spared for another full year.

■ Does the abbess's letter suggest to you that the commissioners were using (a) gentle persuasion and incentives, or (b) bullying pressure?

Not all the great abbeys were closed peacefully. The abbot of Woburn and the prior of Lenton were arrested for treason and were executed, along with several monks and four Lenton labourers, in 1538. Another three abbots were hanged in 1539: those of Colchester and Reading for their opposition to religious change, and the abbot of Glastonbury for hiding away 'as much plate and adornment as would have sufficed to have begun a new abbey'. A new law was made by Parliament in 1539 to confirm that the closures already made were legal, and to set a pattern for those which were still open.

■ Imagine that you are the head of a religious house in 1538. Reason out what would be your best course of action, taking into account your own religious beliefs, your future welfare and that of your monks or nuns.

The great land-grab

As soon as the closure of the monasteries began there was a rush of people anxious to get hold of their huge estates. In 1537 Valle Crucis was leased, or let for a period of years, to a Yorkshire squire, Sir William Pickering. He sub-let it to two other tenants, but the lease stayed with the Pickerings. His son complained in 1573:

> certain persons in Wales do by secret means go about to bring to pass ... the purchasing of certain lands, belonging to the dissolved Monastery of Valle Crucis, which ... I have in farm of the Queen's Majesty for many years yet continuing;
>
> Letter from Sir William Pickering (son) to Lord Burghley, 22 January 1573

Valle Crucis ruins in 1823

Artists' views, like this one, made the abbey a tourist spot from the eighteenth century onwards.

The demand to buy these estates was enormous. A few generations later the whole business was seen by one writer in this way:

> All the *revenues* of these ... religious houses, were under the government of this new Court of Augmentations, which being no sooner planted, began ... to flourish and bear plenty of fruit, whereby not only they that therewith were daily fed but as many as could smell thereof were in short time fattened. Many who before ... [had been] servants ... were shortly Masters.
>
> From *A Chronicle and Defence of the English Reformation*, after 1600

incomes

■ What were the results of the Dissolution, according to this writer?

What really happened? The figures, or *statistics*, on the next page will give you some idea of the wealth that changed hands when the monasteries were closed down.

An aerial view of the site of Margam Abbey, West Glamorgan

Religious houses in England and Wales 1534	848
Religious houses closed by order 1536–40	c560
Yearly income from their estates	£132,000
Value of abbey treasure confiscated	£85,000
Sales of abbey treasure, lead etc	£15,000

Grants of land by Henry VIII
    sale grants   1,524   (95.6%)
    give-away grants   69   (4.4%)
	1,593

Government income from abbey property in 1544 (sales, rents, tithes etc)	£253,292
Percentage of abbey lands sold by 1547	66%

1 How did Henry VIII dispose of most of the land which went into private hands during his reign?

2 You have seen how much income the government was getting from the abbeys in 1544. Was the income likely to stay as high as that?

Margam Abbey in Glamorgan was bought by the powerful Mansel family in 1540 for £938 6s 8d. Part of the abbey was converted into a house in 1552 but this was pulled down in 1780. A huge orangery – a stone-built hothouse for tropical fruit – was built on the abbey site in 1787. It can be seen in the aerial photograph above. Nearby you can see the remains of the chapter house, where the roof collapsed in 1799. The abbey church which can be seen through the trees, is now the parish church. A new stately home, called Margam Castle, was built between 1830 and 1835, further away from the estate cottages which clustered around the old abbey site. Other abbey buildings in Wales were put to industrial use. Neath Abbey site was used for smelting copper, and an iron foundry and wire works were set up on land that had belonged to Tintern Abbey.

The hall of the Charterhouse, London, a Carthusian abbey turned into a charity hospital by a private owner who had bought it from the Crown

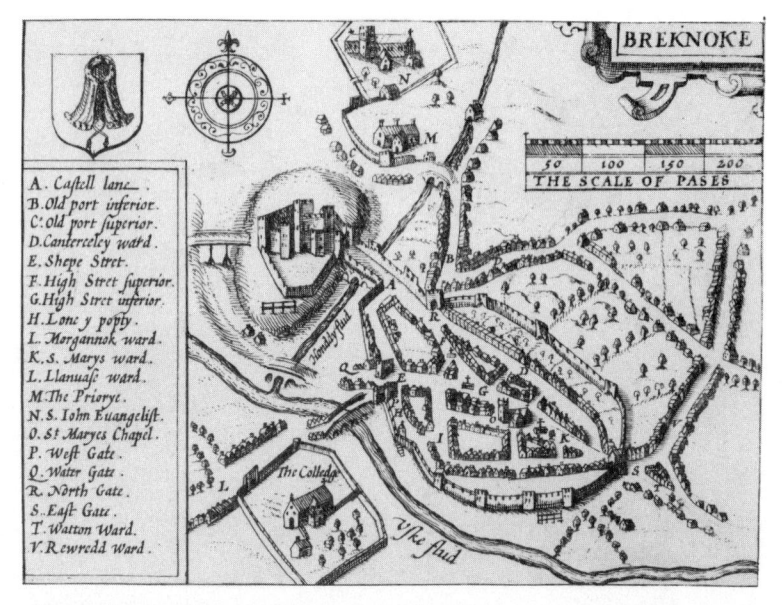

Christ College, Brecon, Powys, drawn c1610
The property of a Dominican friary was used in 1542 to set up a college where clergymen held a school. The school belongs to the Church in Wales today.

But did all the abbey wealth go to private owners in this way? Were there no plans to help the public in general with some of it? One rumour which was going around in 1536 is mentioned in a letter sent to Lord Lisle, an important official:

> it is thought that all houses worth under 300 marks shall be suppressed and *had* to the King's use for the maintenance of certain notable persons in learning and good qualities about his Highness.

put

Letter by William Popley to Lord Lisle, 9 March 1536

Simon Fish, in his protest pamphlet in 1528 had said:

> Divers of your noble predecessors, kings of this realm, have given lands to monasteries to give a certain sum of money yearly to the poor people, whereof for the ancient of the time, they give never one penny ... wherefore if your grace will build a sure hospital that shall never fail to relieve us, all your poor *bedemen*, so take from them all these things.

people receiving aid

Supplication of the Beggars by Simon Fish, 1528

The statistics below show what the government did to improve religion and education in the kingdom with monastic money:

New bishops appointed (with ex-abbey churches as cathedrals)	6
Cathedral grammar schools financed	11
University colleges set up	2
University professors appointed	10

The money spent in this way was only a small part of the income the crown made. Most of it was spent on Henry VIII's wars in the 1540s.

Out of the cloisters

A nineteenth-century picture of Syon nunnery being closed down in 1539

Is the artist trying to make you feel a certain way about what was happening? How is this done?

What happened to the monks, nuns and friars after the Dissolution? There have been many different views about this, as the following remarks show:

> It is a lamentable thing to see a legion of monks and nuns, who have been chased from their monasteries, wandering miserably hither and thither, seeking means to live, and several honest men have told me that what with monks,

nuns, and persons dependent on the monasteries suppressed, there were over 20,000 who knew not how to live.

Ambassador Eustace Chapuys, 8 July 1536

Richard bishop of Dover... was in Gloucester, and there... in the houses of friars... put the said friars *at their liberty*, whether they would continue in their houses and keep their religion and *injunctions*... or else give up their houses into the king's hands... as the world is now they were not able to keep them and live in their houses, wherefore voluntarily they gave their houses into the visitor's hands to the king's use... the visitor took their houses, and charitably delivered them, and gave them letters to visit their friends, and so go to other houses, with the which they were very well content, and so departed.

let them choose rules

Report by the Mayor and Aldermen of Gloucester, 28 July 1538

■ Look at the modern painting opposite of the closure of Syon Nunnery. Is there anything about the picture which makes you think the artist sympathises (a) with the nuns, or (b) the suppressors?

Historians have found out a lot about what really happened from the official papers kept at the time. There are lists of pensions paid after monasteries were closed and a register kept by the Archbishop of Canterbury's officials, as well as parish records and the wills of individuals who had been monks or nuns. What do these documents show? The total number of 'religious', which includes monks, nuns and friars, was about 10,689 in 1534. During the closure of the smaller abbeys in 1536 they were offered either pensions, or permission to become priests in the community or to move to one of the remaining religious houses. When the larger houses were closed, transfer to other houses was no longer possible. Most of the religious who left after November 1537 were given pensions. The pensions varied a lot, as these figures from Yorkshire show:

Pensioner	Annual Income of House	Annual Pension
	£	£ s d
Abbot of Fountains	1,000	100 0 0
Abbot of Whitby	419	66 13 4
Prioress of Nunmonkton	75	13 6 8
Prioress of Nunburnholme	6	3 6 8
Abbot of Selby	739	100 0 0
5 senior monks of Selby	—	8 0 0
6 senior monks of Selby	—	6 0 0
9 junior monks of Selby	—	5 0 0
2 novices of Selby	—	2 13 5

G W O Woodward

One strange fact, however, is that about 1,900 had no help at all. None of the 1,041 friars received pensions and 86 nuns are known to have been unpensioned. What became of them? For the men there were a number of possibilities. They could become priests in parish churches or in chantries. These were private chapels paid for by wealthy families where prayers were said for dead relatives. Some might become family chaplains – live-in priests who held daily services for the members of a rich household. Others could become private tutors to the children of a nobleman or squire. The ability to read and write could enable some to become clerical workers. Only small pieces of evidence about individual monks can be found in the documents, such as this item about four monks from Wales:

> 10 April 1537: Thomas Piell, recently monk of Tintern [Gwent], Llandaff diocese, *dispensation* [permission] to hold a *benefice* [become a parish priest] and *change of habit* [change from monk's clothing to that of a priest]. Also William Hopkyns, Thomas Robyns, William Machyn; Suppressed [the abbey].
>
> From an official register kept by the Archbishop of Canterbury's staff

With so many leaving the monasteries at the same time, it must have been very difficult for them all to find work. Government commissioner John London sent this message to Cromwell:

> Now they be dismissed out of their houses no man will admit any of them to be *curates* [parish priest's assistant], unless they do bring their *capacities* [licences]; wherefore I beseech your lordship we may have them with speed, for in the meantime the poor men be without livings, and now I have *set many abroad* [sent many away].
>
> Letter from Dr John London to Cromwell, 6 November 1538

Tintern Abbey ruins in moonlight, c1800

What about the nuns? They were in a very difficult position. Women were not allowed to be priests, so the former nuns very often had to go to live with relatives. Henry VIII did not release the nuns, or monks, from their vow of chastity, though some nuns are known to have married, but very little information exists about any of them. One historian found that in Lincolnshire eighteen out of the known total of sixty-one ex-nuns eventually married (29.5 per cent). Nuns' pensions were lower than those for monks, usually between £2 and £3. At Godstow, the tough Abbess Bulkeley was granted a pension of £50 a year. Out of the twenty who lived there, sixteen nuns were pensioned. In Wales the small nunneries of Llanllŷr (Dyfed) and Llanllugan (Powys) were less fortunate. Their prioresses, Elizabeth Benham at Llanllŷr and Rose Lewys at Llanllugan, got only £4 and £3 respectively.

So they all went their separate ways; the monks, nuns and friars from hundreds of abbeys, great and small. The break-up was sometimes harsh and sometimes quite sympathetic. But it often came very suddenly, like a storm out of the blue. Benedictine monk John Alcester wrote this note on the last page of an abbey copy of the Bible in 1540:

> And the year of Our Lord [1540] the monastery of Evesham was suppressed by King Henry VIII... the 30 day of January at evensong time, the convent being in their choir at this verse: *'Deposuit potentes...'* And they would not *suffer* them to make an end. Philip Hawford being abbot at that time and 30 were at that day alive in the said monastery.
>
> Note in Bible from Evesham Monastery, 1540

Latin for: he casts down the powerful

allow

Soon silence settled on the cloisters: the long silence of 'bare ruin'd choirs where late the sweet birds sang'. You can still sense it today if you visit the ruins – Fountains, Tintern, Glastonbury – or leafy Valle Crucis amid the hills of North Wales.

A quiet scene by the lake at Valle Crucis

Find out more for yourself

1. How many monastic houses were there in your own county? You can find this out from an Ordnance Survey map (the 1:50000 Scale Series). Ancient ruins and buildings are marked in old-style lettering, and those under state care are marked as shown in the margin. You can find out details about the most famous ones by looking under the abbey's name in an encyclopaedia or in one of the books listed below.

2. Are there places connected with former monasteries in your district? Some place-names can give clues to a link with the abbeys: names which include the words 'monk', 'nun', 'abbey', 'abbot', 'priory', and 'grange', for instance. Here are some examples: Nunthorpe (North Yorkshire), Milton Abbot (Devon), Nuneaton (Warwickshire), Monks Horton (Kent), Prior Park (Cumbria), Grangetown (Cardiff, South Glamorgan), Grange of Lindores (Fife). In Wales the word *mynach* (monk) appears in some place-names, and the word *ysbyty* (hospital) in a Welsh place-name usually means an old monastic hospital.

3. Write a script of an official visitation to a monastic house, with dialogue for two or three visiting commissioners and for members of the house being interviewed one by one. Any important announcement would be made to the whole community.

These books will help you find out more about abbeys:

D Knowles and R N Hadcock, *Medieval Religious Houses* (Longman, 1971)

G M Wright, *Discovering Abbeys and Priories* (Shire Publications, 1976)

Abbeys: An Illustrated Guide to Ancient Monuments (HMSO)

There are also the following useful maps:

Map of Monastic Britain (two sheets), (Ordnance Survey, 1978)

P Hendry and J McWilliam, *Cathedrals and Abbeys Map of the British Isles* (Bartholomew Historic Map Series, c1976)

Ordnance Survey 1:50000 Scale Map Series

The Ordnance Survey Atlas of Great Britain (Ordnance Survey/Hamlyn, 1982)

(Dates are for latest editions.)

Index

Aske, Robert   40-1

Benedict, Saint   6, 9, 10
Boleyn, Anne   34-6
Brereton, Sir William   23
Bulkeley, Abbess   42, 48
Bury Abbey   13, 39

Comperta   30-2
Cromwell, Thomas   2, 21, 24, 26, 28-31, 35, 39, 42, 48
Cymer Abbey   23, 32

Fish, Simon   19, 21, 45
Furness Abbey   41, 42

Glastonbury Abbey   12, 33, 43, 49
Godstow Abbey   42, 48

Henry VIII   1, 2, 20-3, 26-9, 30, 34, 36-7, 42, 44-5, 48-9

Kingston, Sir William   35-6

Monks' horarium   8

Neath Abbey   2, 3, 23

Pilgrimage of Grace   40-1

Rievaulx Abbey   5, 11, 13
Roche Abbey   38
Rochford, Lord   35, 36

Salusbury, Abbot   22-5, 32

Thomas, Abbot Leyshon   3, 23
Tintern Abbey   45, 48, 49

Valle Crucis   2, 4-5, 7, 11, 15-18, 22-5, 32, 34-7, 43, 49
Valor Ecclesiasticus   15, 30

Welsh poets   2, 3, 14, 17
Wolsey, Cardinal   19, 22

Acknowledgements

The author and publishers are grateful to the following for permission to reproduce material:

Aerofilms Ltd, page 44; BBC Hulton Picture Library, pages 5 and 39; BBC Hulton Picture Library and Bettmann, pages 19 and 21; B T Batsford Ltd, pages 16, 19 and 26; British Library, pages 5, 6, 9, 11, 14, 20, 23, 24, 45 and 48; Trustees of the British Museum, page 22; City of Bristol Museum and Art Gallery, page 46; Conway Library, Courtauld Institute of Art, and F H Crossley and M H Ridgway, pages 13 and 41; President and Fellows of Corpus Christi College, Oxford, page 15; © Crown Copyright, Reproduced with the permission of the Controller of Her Majesty's Stationery Office, page 3; © Crown Copyright, English Heritage, page 38; *Country Life*, page 45; Fitzwilliam Museum, Cambridge, page 12; Frick Collection, New York, page 26; Longman Group Ltd, page 25; Mansell Collection, pages 27 and 37; Mansell Collection and Alinari, page 9; Mary Evans Picture Library, pages 7, 35 and 40; National Museum of Wales, page 2; National Portrait Gallery, page 34; President and Council of the Royal College of Surgeons of England and Courtauld Institute of Art, page 29; Royal Commission on Ancient and Historical Monuments in Wales, pages 17, 18, 34 and 43; Royal Commission on Historical Monuments in England, page 14; © Scala/Firenze, page 27; Somerset Rural Life Museum, page 33; Trustees of the Wallace Collection, London, page 28; Walters Art Gallery, page 10; Wayland Publishers Ltd, pages 4 and 7.

The picture on the front cover is a detail from J M W Turners' painting of Valle Crucis in 1794, reproduced with the permission of the Trustees of the British Museum.

Every attempt has been made to contact copyright holders, but we apologise if any have been overlooked.

A World of Change

This book is part of a series entitled *A World of Change*, intended for the 11–14 age group. The aim of the whole series is to combine a firm framework of historical fact with a 'skill-based' approach. The factual content provides continuity, and the opportunity to study causation and development. It is balanced by the two other vital ingredients for lively study of history: opportunity for 'empathy', which enables children to make an imaginative leap into the past; and study of a variety of original sources, both written and visual.

The series comprises a core textbook which studies a number of themes important in the Early Modern Age, approximately 1450–1700; a number of linked topic books; and a teacher's book for the whole series (which includes copyright-free worksheets).

The core book is primarily concerned with the British Isles, but within the context of what was happening in the rest of the world, known and unknown. The well-known political, religious and economic themes are considered. So too are the lives of ordinary men, women and children, and the way in which both change and continuity affected them. The book does not set out to be a full chronological survey, but it is hoped that it is sufficiently flexible to be used in that way if desired.

The core textbook is complete in itself, but has also been designed to provide a number of stepping-off points for 'patch studies'. Opportunities for this kind of work are provided by the eight *World of Change* topic books which are clearly linked to the themes in the main book. However, the topic books are also designed so that they can be used on their own if desired. All the topic books are listed on the back cover.

For the teacher

A vast amount of information about monastic houses in Britain can be found in Knowles and Hadcock's indispensable *Medieval Religious Houses* (see page 50). Monastic sites under public guardianship or protection feature in official lists and many are open to the public. In England those in state guardianship are administered by English Heritage, in Wales by Cadw, in Scotland by the Scottish Office's Department of Ancient Monuments and in Northern Ireland by the Northern Ireland Office. Guide books to the historic monuments are published by the supervising agencies — both general books and individual guides to particular sites. Site guides include detailed ground plans.

Some suggestions for useful background reading:

G Baskerville, *English Monks and the Suppression of the Monasteries* (Jonathan Cape, 1937)

A G Dickens, *The English Reformation* (Fontana, 1967)

G Haigh, *The Last Days of the Lancashire Monasteries and the Pilgrimage of Grace* (Chetham Society, 1969)

D Knowles, *The Religious Orders in England: III The Tudor Age* (Cambridge University Press, 1959)

G V Price, *Valle Crucis Abbey* (Hugh Evans & Son, 1952)

Glanmor Williams, *The Welsh Church from Conquest to Reformation,* 2nd Edn (University of Wales Press, 1976)

G W O Woodward, *The Dissolution of the Monasteries* (Blandford, 1966)

J Youings, *The Dissolution of the Monasteries* (George Allen & Unwin, 1971)

© Robert M Morris 1987

All rights reserved. No part of this publication may be reproduced, stored in a retrieval system or transmitted in any form or by any means, electronic, mechanical, photocopying, recording or otherwise, without the prior written consent of the copyright holders. Applications for such permission should be addressed to the publishers: Stanley Thornes (Publishers) Ltd, Old Station Drive, Leckhampton, CHELTENHAM GL53 0DN, England.

First published in 1987 by:
Stanley Thornes (Publishers) Ltd
Old Station Drive
Leckhampton
CHELTENHAM GL53 0DN
England

Typeset by Tech-Set, Gateshead, Tyne & Wear
Printed and bound in Great Britain by
Ebenezer Baylis & Son Ltd, Worcester

British Library Cataloguing in Publication Data

Morris, Robert
　　Bare ruined choirs: the fate of a welsh abbey.
　　1. Abbeys — Wales — History — 16th
　　century
　　I. Title
　　942.9　　　　DA737

ISBN 0-85950-544-8